D0722017

Rebels All!

IDEAS IN ACTION
THOUGHT AND CULTURE IN THE UNITED STATES
SINCE 1945

George Cotkin, Series Editor

Ideas in Action encourages historians to consider large and important topics pertaining to cultural and intellectual life in the United States since 1945. Drawing on the secondary literature surrounding a topic, these books discover and dissect compelling issues related to large cultural questions as they change over time, and they give authors an opportunity to interpret, to speculate, and to "think out loud," while furthering strong critical debate. Books in the series deal not in abstractions but anchor ideas firmly in the context of politics, culture, and society. They are written in a style that is accessible to a wide range of readers and that captures the author's personality and point of view.

Rebels All!

A Short History of the Conservative Mind in Postwar America

KEVIN MATTSON

RUTGERS UNIVERSITY PRESS
New Brunswick, New Jersey, and London

Library of Congress Cataloging-in-Publication Data

Mattson, Kevin, 1966–
    Rebels all! : a short history of the conservative mind in postwar
America / Kevin Mattson.
        p.   cm.
    Includes bibliographical references and index.
    ISBN 978-0-8135-4343-7 (hardcover : alk. paper)
    1. Conservatism—United States—History—20th century.
    2. Conservatism—United States—History—21st century.
    3. United States—Politics and government—1945–1989.
    4. United States—Politics and government—1989–   I. Title.
    JC573.2.U6M354 2008
    320.520973—dc22   2007044891

A British Cataloging-in-Publication record for this book is available
from the British Library.

Visit our Web site: http://rutgerspress.rutgers.edu

Manufactured in the United States of America

In the memory of Christopher Lasch, my teacher . . .
From an apostate, still respectful

The picture today in American politics is of intelligence without force or enthusiasm facing force and enthusiasm without intelligence.

—David Riesman and Nathan Glazer,
"The Intellectuals and Discontented Classes," 1955

Contents

Acknowledgments

Thanks first to George Cotkin. He proposed the idea of writing a small book exploring big ideas from the past, especially those that intersected with politics. He is not only a great series editor but a great historian. Thanks also to Shae Davidson, who helped research this book. He is a young historian in his own right, and his insights about the book have been immensely helpful. So, too, Julian Nemeth, who helped check footnotes and provided marvelous criticisms that went beyond the call of his job. Jennifer Burns read the manuscript and gave very helpful advice as well. My friend Mark Schmitt acted the sage at a very important moment in revision, offering important warnings about my argument. Nelson Lichtenstein provided an excellent and very thoughtful read of the final manuscript. As usual, the typical author caveat should be evoked: any mistake or weakness in this work is my own.

Rebels All!

INTRODUCTION

The Party of Ideas?

> We are the party of ideas.
>
> —George W. Bush, 2000

THESE WORDS ROLLED OFF THE LIPS of a man who calls himself a "gut player." A man who when asked by the conservative journalist Tucker Carlson back in 1999 to name a weakness said: "sitting down and reading a 500-page book on public policy or philosophy or something." A man who later shocked people and made headline news by reading a book by French existentialist Albert Camus. A man who toned down his prep school roots and campaigned as a Texas populist and who, in the words of one journalist, "has been quick about cracks about intellectuals and criticisms of institutions like his own alma mater, Yale University." A man whose own speechwriter called him "uncurious and as a result ill-informed." A man famous for mispronouncing words and looking flummoxed when off-script at press conferences. This president—a man whom many describe as the most anti-intellectual president in postwar America—said he led a party of ideas.[1]

Odd? Not necessarily. It tells us a great deal about the state of conservative ideas today, or at least it *should*. Consider the array of books about President Bush by conservative intellectuals. These men of ideas and arguments portray Bush as a tough-ass rebel, a populist hero, and a president who pisses off the liberal establishment every chance he gets. Case in point: Fred Barnes's book, *Rebel-in-Chief: Inside the Bold and Controversial Presidency of*

George W. Bush, written before Bush plummeted in the polls and
faced the brunt of the midterm elections of 2006. Barnes is one
of America's quintessential conservative intellectuals who gravi-
tated to the *Weekly Standard* during the 1990s and cut his teeth
in the scream-fest of cable television talk shows. As his book title
suggests, Barnes does not see Bush as a statesman (or as stately);
rather, his idealized president looks like Marlon Brando mounting his motorcycle and raising hell in the iconic 1953 film *The
Wild One*. For Barnes, Bush is "defiant of the press, scornful of
the conventional wisdom, and keen to reverse or at least sub-
stantially reform long-standing policies." The president is "edgy"
and "blunt"; he leads an "army of insurgents." He has, like most
rebels, a "cool optimism" and "pugnacity" at the same time. He
is certain of his cause and ready to clash with a conformist society scared of change; he is a rebel intent on remaking the world
according to his own ideals, possessing an authenticity society
might fail to understand but that right-wing intellectuals like
Barnes *adore*. He appears, it would seem, as the true inheritor of
the radical and utopian spirit emanating from the 1960s. And, as
a onetime colleague of Barnes put it, President Bush has pioneered this style of rebellion all the while driving "liberals"—
meaning those fuddy-duds and establishment types—"insane."[2]

This populist aggression is found everywhere among conservatives, not just among intellectuals touting the president's verve.
Indeed, the aggressiveness is hard to miss no matter where you
turn. It emanates from the airwaves every time Rush Limbaugh,
Michael Savage, or Sean Hannity get on to thump their arguments
out. You watch it in the crazy world of political talk shows on
cable television—with Bill O'Reilly's and Ann Coulter's acerbic
style. And any quick look at recent conservative book titles suggests the same: *Liberalism Kills Kids*; *The Party of Death: The
Democrats, the Media, the Courts, and the Disregard for Human Life*;
*Liberal Fascism: The Secret History of the American Left, from Mussolini
to the Politics of Meaning*; *Godless: The Church of Liberalism*; and

The Enemy at Home: The Cultural Left and Its Responsibility for 9/11. These titles indicate that conservative writers still see themselves— even after conservatives have won every level of political office in the United States during the early twenty-first century, created numerous conservative media outlets, and turned the Supreme Court in a conservative direction—as embattled populists ready to combat a monstrously powerful liberal elite. *Rebels all.*

Conservative style today is tough, brash, and by many accounts, not very *conservative* sounding. After all, isn't conservatism supposed to be about maintaining standards, upholding civility, and frowning on rebellion? There is a distinctly *American* feel to Bush and his intellectual defenders. The style is obviously populist, its pizzazz and brashness playing well to a culture of entertainment, to an audience ready to boo and jeer more than listen contemplatively. Though it purports to be traditionalist, this brand of conservatism seems more inclined to embrace rebellion and to throw away the old order. It is "bold" and daring in its pronouncements and profoundly distrustful of intellectual sophistication, typically seen as a cover for elitism or simply the doubtfulness of sissies unwilling to embrace risk. At the same time, it loves power and a sense that the world can be remade when power is acquired. It is aggressive, confrontational, and strangely utopian.

The style seems so confrontational, so—dare I say it?—akin to student protestors of the 1960s who marched with self-righteousness and self-assuredness that they were bringing utopian transformation to America. It is the party of conservatives today—not the Left—that has inherited the spirit of rebellion born during the sixties. Take President Bush and his boldest move ever. When he announced the invasion of Iraq, he seemed to suggest to Americans: *Yes, we can go into Iraq and create a perfect democracy, a new city on the hill in the Middle East, without even working very hard at it.* But it did not stop there; there was a domestic side to this vision. Bush the rebel suggested: *Yes, we can cut taxes while avoiding deficits and still fund the military. Yes, all would prosper if we had a society of free markets and small government (the ownership society), as human nature tends toward the good, and all will do well without help or assistance or any of those meddling social programs. Yes, we can remake the world with the ideals of democracy and freedom first and foremost.* Those who doubt such things are cynics lacking moral insight, naysayers stuck in the rut of reason, or those holding up progress with their sideways and backward glances.

Bush's infectious utopianism explains the weirdest act of intellectual apostasy during the Iraq War—the self-transformation of Christopher Hitchens from revolutionary socialist to Bush supporter. Though berated by the Left today as a drunken buffoon, he is an iconic symbol for our times, especially in the world of ideas and politics. Hitchens, once a writer for the *Nation* who denounced Bill Clinton as too centrist, finds himself now supporting the Iraq War and rubbing elbows with fanatical conservatives like David Horowitz and Grover Norquist, as well as the editorial board of the *Weekly Standard*. The transition is not so strange as some would think. After all, Hitchens described missing the "Paris uprisings of 1968" as "a big regret of my life." Now he feels he can live that revolutionary enthusiasm in the quick deposing of Saddam Hussein and the utopian dream of a democracy springing forth out of tyranny overnight. He reported loving the sound of gunfire in the streets of Baghdad after Hussein's sons were found dead; no doubt, it reminded him of the students and workers throwing rocks at the cops and denouncing the French government and higher education bureaucracies in 1968. His full-throated cry in support of the war, even as late as 2006, suggests that the true spirit of the 1960s lives more on the Right today than it does on the Left. To become a radical utopian thinker, you must move right—to where the radicalism and utopianism seem to be happening.[3]

So, the conservative of today is a utopian rebel. And this too: today's conservatives see themselves as hip and cool, taking their cues, as does Bush, from Marlon Brando more than from the man in the gray flannel suit. During the 1960s, Nathan Glazer could refer to the "hip conservatism of the *National Review.*" Such a statement might have sounded odd back then, but not today. Numerous liberal critics complain that conservatives have overpowered the Left by being more humorous and cool. John Powers, for instance, once called the conservative *Weekly Standard* "breezy," with "enjoyable writers" and "funny articles." The prospect of reading the left-wing *Nation,* on the other hand, feels "less like a treat than an obligation" to him. Echoing this sentiment, conservative critics today write entire books about how they enjoy watching *South Park* or wearing hip clothing; others treasure trendy health foods and organic coffee. Hipness and coolness, like rebellion, are no longer the property of the Left. George W. Bush's Marlon Brando is echoed in the conservative movement's numerous James Deans—the grassroots "hipublicans."[4]

Conservative intellectuals today can even sound "postmodern," making arguments that you would expect from an English professor stoked up on deconstruction and relativism. For instance, David Horowitz, the key organizer behind a "student bill of rights" that would empower state legislatures to police classroom content for liberal indoctrination, does not sound conservative when he talks about defending right-wing students from left-wing bias on U.S. college campuses. He talks about "diversity." To justify his initiative, Horowitz writes as follows: "Human knowledge is a never-ending pursuit of the truth" because "there is no humanly accessible truth that is not in principle open to challenge, and that no party or intellectual faction has a monopoly on wisdom."[5] When conservatives argue against evolution being taught exclusively in schools and in favor of intelligent design (ID) today, they too sound rather postmodern. It's all about offering different "paradigms" to students. The leading intellectual exponent who argues that ID should be taught equally with evolution, points out that his thinking is "dead-bang mainstream" in "academia these days."[6] Both Horowitz and the ID proponents rebel against the oppression of liberal hegemony, and they sound like the hipster literary critics who populate America's English departments.

The Good Ole Days?

This new style of rebel conservatism must have burst forth in the 1990s, or so some might think. Numerous observers on the Right have argued that Bush has perverted conservatism from what it once was. Listen, for instance, to Jeffrey Hart. He is a man of reserve, prudence, and humility, and he does not like what he sees in the presidency of Bush. He wrote a fine book about the history of conservative ideas, focusing his attention, right-fully, on the *National Review* and its editor, William F. Buckley. Toward the end of the book, he worries openly about Bush's "military Wilsonianism" and an evangelical dogmatism that hopes to remake the world. For Hart, as for some other conservatives, Bush's policies are not really conservative. With his command of the past, Hart finds it easy to tell a tale of declension. Put simply, the tale goes thus: We conservatives were once great in the golden, early days of the *National Review* when we had good ideas, and now we have fallen. Hart then made this implicit claim explicit in a recent piece, written for a liberal magazine. Here he argues that Bush's desire to remake the world misses the point of William Buckley's more intellectually principled "conservatism" that defined itself, following the teaching of the great European social philosopher Edmund Burke, as a "politics of reality." Hart chafes at the utopian and ideological ideas expounded by America's rebel-in-chief.[7]

Hart's argument resonates because it is part of a mantra heard on the Right. More and more conservatives are recoiling from George W. Bush, especially after the midterm elections dealt him a serious blow or at least made his lame duck presidency lamer.

There is now a growing chorus of voices that suggest something called a "conservative soul" has been lost, that declension explains all. The talk is of "hijacking." Christine Todd Whitman, Andrew Sullivan, and John Dean offer us this story of declension—a tale of falling from an original state of conservative grace. They act taken aback by the stridency of today's conservative movement and Bush's utopian radicalism. They recoil from the brash tones of Ann Coulter who thumbs her nose at civility. John Dean writes: "Contemporary conservatives have become extremely contentious, confrontational, and aggressive in nearly every area of politics and governing." The backdrop to such a statement is that it was not always so. There was a time when the conservative soul was brighter and healthier. Andrew Sullivan, for instance, suggests he is "rescuing conservatism" from its present ill-conceived fate.[8]

The declension thesis just does not work, however. There is no betrayal of the conservative mind or soul going on today. We are witnessing instead an indigenous form of conservative thinking started more than fifty years ago that, since then, has become a permanent feature of what I will call the postwar conservative mind. Let me offer a brief example to make my point: consider a quick comparison of Ann Coulter and William Buckley. Coulter is the Right's most noticed pundit today, whose books sell out when they hit the shelves; Buckley is the most important and high-profile intellectual, whose influence, following Hart's own analysis, peaked in the 1950s and 1960s when the magazine he formed, *National Review*, was in its salad days. If Hart is right, you might expect a gulf between them. Coulter would play the ideological and utopian fanatic to Buckley's staid and aristocratic conservatism and "politics of reality." Such an interpretation could follow from the fact that Coulter was fired from Buckley's magazine for being too controversial.

For sure, there is a difference between the two thinkers. Coulter is more snarky, and Buckley is more pleasant. Coulter is more ignorant, Buckley is more learned. Buckley had drawn together a group of conservative thinkers to form the *National Review* when conservatives were not as popular as they are now. It is hard to imagine Coulter worrying about alliances or much of anything besides her own popularity. And it is hard to imagine Buckley saying something as wild as Coulter did about the war on terror and America's appropriate attitude toward Muslims: "We should invade their countries, kill their leaders and convert them to Christianity." This too: Coulter, as much as she might think otherwise, has benefited from the 1960s, including the decade's feminism and even the decade's countercultural rebellion (she was, after all, once a Deadhead, the perfect icon of the countercultural past). And yet, with all of this in mind, Coulter is best understood as pushing the intellectual inheritance she got from Buckley one step further to make it fit a new popular culture.[9]

Buckley pioneered the conservative style of going for shock—for saying things that made readers blush. In writing *God and Man at Yale*, his first, controversial book, Buckley pooh-poohed the "so-called conservative" who was "uncomfortably disdainful of controversy." The book argued, from the perspective of a student who had recently graduated, that certain Yale professors should be "discharged" and that academic freedom was merely a "superstition" that merited little concern. Buckley could brush such temperate thinking aside and call for the overthrow of a well-established practice at one of America's oldest higher education institutions—again eliciting the idea of the conservative as rebel more than as defender of the status quo. He was ready and willing to wage war on his elders. He quoted Arthur Koestler, who encouraged people to "write ruthlessly" and then said he was not worried about the "the antagonism" his book would "evoke." Buckley knew and was right in knowing that to call for revolutionary change at Yale would paint him as a "radical" and young upstart. So be it, he suggested, because "too many conservatives are holding back because they regard as futile the espousal of any radical measure." In many ways, Buckley's spirit drew from a culture in which young, white males stood disaffected from a conformist and complacent society during a decade that produced Brando and Dean and the Beats as much as men in gray flannel suits. Buckley's message to future conservatives was this: be bold, shocking, daring, and rebellious. America's public sphere courted controversy and wildness, values that would seem to rub up against a Burkean intellectual upholding dignified and civilized discussion. And so Buckley fired a shot heard throughout the history of the conservative mind.[10]

Playing to the loud and cacophonous feeling of American popular culture has served the conservative mind well. The liberal journalist James Wechsler, who debated Buckley a great deal during the 1950s, described their act as one of "vaudeville performers" for cheering and booing crowds.[11] The persona was solidified when Buckley created *Firing Line*, the first true pundit talk show on television back in 1966. Buckley's model suggested that conservative intellectuals should dish out shocking and explosive fare for a culture of entertainment that would only continue to demand more. And Buckley bequeathed such a role to Coulter.

Coulter's "vaudeville" performance has become so extreme and so shaped by the blitzkrieg world of cable television that many are not sure if they should take her seriously. After all, most intellectuals are not so quick as to design their own action figure doll. Not so Coulter. When you pull the string, the doll repeats statements she made in the past, such as: "I think we ought to nuke North Korea right now just to give the rest of the world a warning. Boom!" or "We need to execute people like John Walker [Lindh] in order to physically intimidate liberals." As *Time* magazine pointed out, "Coulter goes on actual news programs and deploys so much sarcasm and hyperbole that she sounds more like Dennis Miller than Limbaugh." Her extreme stance and performative style *constitute* her intellectual substance. We witness in Coulter the culmination of the conservative intellectual movement, the "vaudeville" performance updated for the postmodern present. But, no matter what Hart suggests, reading back from Coulter to Buckley is not as difficult as some might think.[12]

Coulter and Buckley's shared style is remarkable enough. But consider also their shared substantive concerns. They pressed themselves into similar intellectual corners. Both wrote books that, against liberal critics, defended Senator Joseph McCarthy's search for communists. Both embraced McCarthy's gruff attack-form of political combat, the tough guy taking it to the effete snobs and communists. Buckley scoffed at liberal characterizations of McCarthy's "reign of terror." Coulter echoed the sentiment in her book *Treason* and turned it up a notch. Both Buckley and Coulter described liberals as vicious attack dogs in a way that sounded vicious itself. Or else they attacked liberals as elitists who refused to debate their opponents but gave little reason to believe that they wanted to debate more than they wanted to throttle their enemies. Buckley could say that "American Liberals are reluctant to co-exist with anyone on their Right." The statement does not sound all that different from Coulter's arguing in *Slander* that "liberals don't try to win arguments, they seek to destroy their opponents and silence dissident opinions." Reading Coulter does not differ from reading Buckley as much as those who espouse declension might suppose. For sure, Coulter is more zany and confrontational, but she appears in other ways just louder and more hysterical, more appropriate for a world of blogs and cable television—a world that came after Buckley's heyday but whose birth could certainly be seen in his own brainchild, *Firing Line*.[13]

Buckley and Coulter's similarities encapsulate a major theme in this book. Realizing that the intellectual terrain has changed, one can say that something called a conservative mind has persisted throughout the years with some incessant features. This is a book that contains a tale both of continuity and change. Things like rebellious anti-intellectualism remain throughout, but an emphasis on evangelical religion grows stronger as we move toward the present. Apocalyptic rhetoric is there from the first years after World War II, but that rhetorical style amps itself up as the world of cable television and blogs becomes more of a reality. The conservative mind acted on history, remaining steadfast, but it was also acted on *by* history, changing in certain ways.

It might sound unfashionable to write about a conservative mind—something that sounds too metaphysical for our ears. Many would suggest a trendier term like "discourse." But the term "mind" is more appropriate for what I want to describe here. The conservative mind, with its synapses and capacity for holding together disparate ideas, is just what I want to discuss here. As historians like George Nash have shown, the conservative mind is made up of divergent beliefs, including free-market libertarianism, traditional beliefs in religion, and a belief that the United States must act aggressively in the world. The conservative mind holds these divergent values throughout the postwar period in American history and welds them together into a unity—a unity of conflict and tension but a unity nonetheless. It provides a scaffolding on which dreams and hopes for the future are hung.[14]

THE CONSERVATIVE MIND AND
AMERICAN EXCEPTIONALISM

Buckley pioneered the conservative mind and Coulter has perfected it, making it fit the increasingly brash tones of our contemporary popular culture. What critics like Hart pine for, in contrast, is a conservatism that draws on Edmund Burke, a conservatism of wisdom and tradition deeply rooted in a European context, the sort of conservatism that he is correct in assuming

George W. Bush knows very little about. It is a conservatism that others have dreamed about. Russell Kirk, for instance, seemed to yearn for it at moments. But it is the sort of conservatism that has never taken hold in America and the sort of conservatism that even Russell Kirk, as we will see, did not really hold to all the time. That's because it is a conservatism that could never work in a country where populism, democracy, and showboating entertainment are too much a part of the national identity.

It is old hat to say that America does not have the tradition or hierarchical features that Europe did and therefore cannot reproduce its style of conservatism. Liberals reminded readers of the point when criticizing Buckley and his fellow conservatives at the *National Review* during the 1950s. But what the criticism misses is how this very lack of tradition and hierarchy is a *constitutive element* of the conservative mind that *has* in fact grown up in the United States. An American love of the new and of the rebellious and confrontational (impossible to miss in our popular culture today) is a foundational feature of the nation's conservative mind. And the conservative mind has even helped contribute to the making of this culture by trying to build on it and by adding to its rebellious and populist disdain for serious and civilized argument. After all, conservatives too have learned the art of thumbing their noses at authority and cheering and booing on demand.

To get a sense of conservative dynamism, consider how many right-wing intellectuals—including some who might have wanted to become the American equivalent of Edmund Burke— are the furthest thing from traditionalists themselves. Their own lives reflect radical dynamism and change. This is clearest in a repeated narrative of conservative intellectual biography—a move from radical left to radical right. Extremism becomes the only constant for many conservative intellectuals; the virtue of vigor wins out over all others. Consider the first generation of postwar conservatives: Whittaker Chambers, Frank Meyer,

James Burnham, and Willmoore Kendall. All of them would become editors at the *National Review* (and will be discussed in chapter 1), and all moved from communism to conservatism. Or consider the neoconservatives of the 1960s and 1970s, many of them beginning as Trotskyists during the 1930s (Irving Kristol, the editor of the *Public Interest*) or "new radicals" in the 1950s (Norman Podhoretz, the editor of *Commentary*). Also consider a later generation: David Horowitz (who compared himself to Chambers) and Peter Collier, as well as the editor of *First Things*, John Richard Neuhaus. All of them embraced radical politics during the 1960s and now are born-again conservatives. That is why their conservatism sounds like a carryover from their past; the *style* of 1960s rebellion serves as an excellent vessel for conservative ideas. Horowitz's move from endorsing the Black Panther Party to saying that blacks should be grateful about slavery because it brought them to America—that trajectory serves conservative intellectuals well today. A penchant for shock is part of the conservative mind and a central feature of its makeup, producing a willingness to become "men of apocalypsis," a term Arthur Schlesinger Jr. applied to conservatives during the Cold War.[15]

This book assumes that conservative arguments have played a role throughout the American past, even though they became much more important in the postwar period. To say this is to give conservatives their due credit. I have heard numerous conservatives complain that they have been excluded from the central narrative of our country's past, their contributions ignored. That should no longer be allowed to happen. But it comes at a critical price to people like Jeffrey Hart and those bemoaning the death of a "conservative soul." For to say that the conservative mind should be at the center of American history is also to say that conservatism has ingested central features of American culture: a love of the new and rebellious, a distrust of sophistication and intellectualism, an embrace of populism that makes "the people" the basis of all things good, a love of popular culture and its penchant for sensation and celebrity over substance. And to put the conservative mind at the center of American history—to see how it both creates and is transformed by American popular culture—is to see new contradictions and problems. To understand these contradictions and problems is central to the story I tell here.

To say that conservatism is central to American history can still pose problems for American historiography. After all, we have inherited a historical myth from the 1950s and 1960s that there really was no conservatism in postwar American history. In 1950, Lionel Trilling famously wrote that "liberalism is not only the dominant but even the sole intellectual tradition" in America. Certainly, Trilling argued, there was a "conservative impulse," but that impulse did not "express" itself "in ideas." Trilling, as we now know, was inaccurate. There were plenty of ideas available on the Right, and they would grow increasingly influential. If Trilling was wrong, New Left critics during the 1960s were even more wrong when they attacked liberalism as if it was the only game in town. For instance, the editors of *Studies on the Left*, one of the leading journals of the New Left, asserted in 1966, two years after Barry Goldwater's run for the presidency, that "liberalism will remain the dominant political ideology of the large corporations and the socially disruptive programs of the ultra-right will continue to be rejected." Rereading this statement makes most of us roll our eyes, realizing, as we do, that these authors would be proven very wrong very soon.[16]

Scholars have worked hard to correct this view of the past. For instance, several recent histories of the 1960s put conservatives smack dead center in the middle of the decade, showing that they were the ultimate victors in the end and that they had been building power for quite some time throughout the decade. This "revisionist" take on the past deserves to be expanded.

Anyone who casts a quick glance realizes that there have *always* been conservative ideas in the past—faith in free markets, religion, and a strong role for the United States abroad. Those ideas were present from the nineteenth century to President Bush's administration today. You can see a streak of conservatism running through American intellectual history—moving, say, from Jonathan Edwards to some anti-Federalists to John Calhoun to the Southern agrarians of the 1930s. But something happened when America crossed over into the postwar period, and it is important to set this out at the beginning of this story.

The conservative mind greeted the postwar years with a feeling of confidence—the sort of confidence that nurtured its radicalism and conviction. There was a belief that political and cultural transformation—even of the most radical kind—was possible. This book opens with a transitional period, when conservatives were first starting to gain that assurance. In the postwar years, there were still some conservative writers who were pessimistic about Americans' ever really accepting their brand of conservatism. Whittaker Chambers, the man who outed Alger Hiss as a communist spy, seemed gloomy about the prospect and still spoke about conservatives preserving "remnants" that might live on but would never attain power. But already by the 1950s, Chambers's attitude seemed old and less relevant than Buckley's optimism. And then by the 1960s, there was no room left to question. Marching ahead with certitude seemed the only legitimate roadmap for the future.

This theme becomes clearer when we compare Buckley and the *National Review* crowd (the foundational period of this story) with the last identifiable prewar conservative movement—the Southern Agrarians. Famous for their collected set of essays, *I'll Take My Stand* (1930), these writers believed that an agrarian way of life, closely associated with the Southland, was superior to industrial capitalism. The latter operated on the basis of science and technology or, more generally, the ideal of progress.

Southern Agrarians like John Crowe Ransom upheld "antique conservatism" that challenged the "progressive" ideal of life. Ransom began his essay in the book with this evocative sentence: "It is out of fashion in these days to look backward rather than forward." But backward these thinkers looked. If their ideals were to be beaten by the machine, they would, as the historian Richard Pells put it, announce "their secession from the dominant assumptions of industrial America." These thinkers seemed reactionary in the deeper sense of that word, hoping to turn the clock back and suspicious that the future was likely not to be promising. If their dreams had to die as remnants, so be it; they would at least have imagined an ideal of the South as a bulwark of conservative ideas—an ideal that would last through the postwar period, but one that would change its tone and hues after the war by standing more firmly and merging with a growing sense of conservative confidence that looked forward more than it looked back.[17]

Richard Weaver would do the most to bring the Southern Agrarian teachings into the postwar period. But he would change them for the times. There was less talk about the South providing an alternative to industrial capitalism, more about how the South could put up a fight against civil rights legislation and the growth of federal power. That after all, was the big crisis conservatives faced during the 1950s. There was a move from the Southern gentleman ideal to the rebel yell in the 1950s. And Richard Weaver would find support for his arguments against the civil rights movement and for Southern resistance in William Buckley, who would push the rebel yell with the conviction that it could transform things for the better. Buckley, the rebel, was no remnant. He was bursting with confidence. The whole purpose behind the *National Review* was to convert the entire community to conservatism. Buckley described how his magazine would aim "at thoughtful people, at opinion makers. We feel that before it is possible to bring the entire nation around politically, we have got to engage the attention of people who for a long time have felt that the conservative position is moribund." To "bring the entire nation around"—that sort of project obviously took confidence, not looking backward nostalgically but forward, energetically and not debilitated with worries.[18]

Dumping the backward glance of the Southern Agrarians, the conservative mind also became more unified and self-conscious, willing to attack liberalism as pervasive and monolithic. With the Cold War, conservative intellectuals like William Buckley ditched their prior isolationist tendencies (which had expressed doubts about America's capacity to do good abroad and thus was a rather gloomy and pessimistic view) for an activist foreign policy. Championing America's role in the world required adopting the eternally optimistic spirit of America too—not the dour doubting of isolationists. Communism demanded muscular aggression; so conservative thinkers argued. By climbing out of the cramped quarters of American isolationism and throwing out nostalgia, conservative intellectuals climbed out of much more as well. The world opened up for them. This is why, as Jeffrey Hart and others continue to point out, William Buckley is so important and why the *National Review* is the beginning of so much to come. Confidence—toughness, assuredness, and a willingness to trust that "the people" were in their camp—became the tone of the conservative mind from that point onward.

That Buckley and the *National Review* serve as the beginning of my story suggests that my story's contours have been traced before. I will not pull any zingers here by dramatically changing the cast of characters that populate existing histories of conservative political thought. A few years ago, some suggested that everything about conservative thinking could be explained by understanding the ideas of Leo Strauss—a name only a few historians and political theorists recognized at the time. As with any claim that a major movement boiled down to one previously obscure name, this was foolish. I will certainly emphasize some figures over others. My intent, though, is to change the lens through which we see the cast of characters we recognize as laying the ground for modern conservatism. This book intends to challenge the way we think about this movement by focusing on certain themes, not new names.[19]

THE CROOKED PATH OF THE CONSERVATIVE MIND

I will begin by examining the founding generation of thinkers gathered around the *National Review*—what is sometimes called the "Old Right." This first generation was free to think about ideas broadly and openly and helped nurture one of the most creative periods in the formation of the postwar conservative mind. My attention then gravitates toward the "neoconservatives" of the mid-1960s and 1970s—a group of thinkers who offered different ways to confront the legacy of the 1960s, one path led by Irving Kristol, the other by Norman Podhoretz, the first rejecting the spirit of that age, the latter more open to the decade's "new sensibility." Neoconservatives are important, and their story needs to be discussed here, but predominantly in terms of how their ideas did not fit the paths trod by the postwar conservative mind up until this point and later. Finally, after the neoconservatives, I turn to the New Right and its intellectuals—with their central credo of populism and their turn back to the path trod by the Old Right—and then finish by examining "postmodern" conservatives, the true inheritors of the utopian, radical, and (in my mind) destructive elements of the 1960s. My particular emphasis here is on prominent, public intellectuals—not academics or lower-profile thinkers. I am as interested in how these intellectuals made their ideas accessible to the wider public as I am in the ideas they were thinking about. To a large extent, I focus on style as much as substance. After all, this is a story that hopes to explain the success and appeal of the movement—that is, how conservative ideas moved to the forefront of the American identity.

Some cautions about this book are in order. Being a book about ideas, this work does not go into great detail about the grassroots movements that were often very important in launching conservative ideas into the mainstream. With that said, these movements *will* be brought into the narrative. After all, the movements clearly informed the intellectual developments (most explicitly Senator Barry Goldwater's grassroots campaign for the presidency in 1964 and then the rise of the New Right during the 1970s). Just like leftist intellectuals, conservative intellectuals hungered for some form of agency that could help transform their ideas into reality. During the 1960s, they obviously got a sense of how this would happen, and so chapter 2 will examine Barry Goldwater's ideas. Chapter 3 will take a quick look at the New Christian Right. Still, my focus throughout this book will be on a project that, though ironically tinged with anti-intellectualism, was still overwhelmingly a project of books, articles, and arguments.

In writing a book about conservative ideas, I am not arguing that these ideas determined history. Conservatives did not seize power from the 1960s onward because of their ideas, no matter what George W. Bush or the funders of the American Enterprise Institute might proclaim. Ideas alone do not win political power; foot soldiers do, and strong candidates and good media campaigns and, most important of all, the right historical conditions (as well as weak political foes). But in pointing this out, some who emphasize politicians and movements take their arguments too far. Public intellectuals on the Right have helped push many ideas into the mainstream, transforming our national discussions in the process. Some critics downplay the role of ideas, forgetting that arguments and ideals *do* matter. And when placed in context, ideas tell us something about a wider movement. So this history of the conservative mind is presented, grandiose as this might sound, as an explanation of conservatism writ large.

Another point about recent treatments of conservative ideas deserves mention here. It has been especially easy to dismiss and even ignore conservative ideas by reducing them to economic self-interest. In numerous political analyses done by the Left and in some intellectual histories of postwar conservatism, emphasis is placed on think tanks and the big money that flows into them. We hear how corporations look for lackeys to provide intellectual heft for tax cuts and procorporate policies. Conservatism is probusiness for sure and is certainly opposed to government regulation on principle, but it is also about cultural ideas and values that need to be taken seriously. It is the conservative mind that weaves these different ideas together. Though money certainly matters to conservative thought and can never be overlooked, ideas and arguments are still about more than money. To argue that conservative ideas are simply a reflection of economic self-interest is a profoundly limited perspective that this book hopes to correct.[20]

With that said, I should make clear my own perspective about the history discussed here and put my own cards on the table. I am a liberal writing a book about conservative ideas. That poses a certain challenge, as I am well aware. Many histories of conservative thought have been written by sympathizers. Perhaps that was necessary. It required partisans to fight for their ideas to be taken seriously. But today, I think liberals must start to engage these ideas themselves. During the 1950s, liberals like Arthur Schlesinger Jr., John Kenneth Galbraith, and James Wechsler debated conservatives like William Buckley, James Burnham, and Whittaker Chambers. Though sometimes fruitless, as Wechsler himself suggested, the dialogue highlighted significant disagreement in American political culture and helped define two important set of ideas. Though it is more difficult to reenergize this debate today, owing to the shrillness of so much conservative rhetoric—one of Coulter's books is titled *How to Talk to a Liberal (if You Must)*—liberals must try. This volume is a small step in that direction.

This book has been written during a period of conservative ascendancy. Though it focuses on how this ascendancy took place—how the conservative mind made itself appealing—it also points to some problems endemic to the conservative mind. As a liberal historian, I will do my best to treat conservative ideas fairly. But I will also make clear what conservatives have gotten wrong about the tradition that I write from—the American liberal tradition. I should point out that I have done the same thing in previous treatments of the radical Left and its criticism of liberalism. I do so because I have never believed that the roles of historian and critic can or should be sharply divided. And this is especially true when one side of a debate has won so much influence over the years. Explanation and criticism should act in concert. My book will treat the intellectual tradition with the level of seriousness it deserves—enough seriousness, I believe, to show where it has succeeded on its own terms and failed on others, and where it has helped transform our view of our political future.

ONE

The First Generation

APOCALYPTIC REBELS WITH A CAUSE

As for me, I will punch anyone who calls me
a conservative in the nose. I am a radical.
—Frank Chodorov, 1956

CERTAIN PREDICTIONS LIVE LONGER than
deserved, even wrong ones. Consider the "end of ideology." An
intellectual forecast about Cold War America, this concept still
provides some historians with a nice tag to hang on the period.
Myth might be a better term for it. Though others had already
expounded the idea, the "end of ideology" was best explained
by Daniel Bell, a respected sociologist and public intellectual.
Bell saw how the "revolutionary impulses of the past century
and a half" collapsed as the terrors of fascism and Stalinism
became undeniable. Ideology had created death camps and
gulags. Millions had died under the reign of terrorist states that
proclaimed the ends justified the means. The sensible conclusion
was, therefore, to shed ideology, to put an "end to chilias-
tic hopes, to millenarianism, to apocalyptic thinking." Ideology
was now a "dead end." No longer would "passion" be a part of
the postwar American mind or taken seriously. Instead, a culture
of complexity and nuance would issue forth in America—a
society that rejected the simplicity of ideology for tougher, more
pragmatic thinking about social and political problem solving.

Bell oscillated between talking prescriptively and descriptively. Sometimes it sounded as if he thought the "end of ideology" was inevitable and at other times that it was a moral imperative. Whatever the case, conservative intellectuals seemed ready to prove him wrong.[1]

The conservative intellectual Russell Kirk seemed, at first, to agree with Daniel Bell. Kirk defined "ideology," a predominantly left-wing phenomenon by the 1950s because it implied communism, as the "product of a priori theories compounded to excuse the envies, resentments, and unhallowed ambitions of rebels against God and man." While opposing ideology, though, Kirk was living on his homestead in Michigan, isolated from the rest of the world and building his own conservative worldview out of traditions from the past that would result in what many would call an ideology. He would label it a "mind" or "program" at times. Whatever it was called, it had revolutionary impulses. He saw the need to "espouse conservatism with the vehemence of a radical. The thinking conservative, in truth, must take on some of the outward characteristics of the radical, today: he must poke about the roots of society, in the hope of restoring vigor to an old tree half strangled in the rank undergrowth of modern passions." So Kirk became a passionate radical jousting with modern passions. Here was a purported enemy of ideology sounding revolutionary and passionate all at once—the conservative paradox *in extremis*.[2]

Kirk was winning fans among conservative intellectuals who were certainly *not* willing to take "passion" out of their own ideas—far from it. Kirk's conservative brethren (and the central cast this chapter deals with) included men like William Buckley, the young editor of the *National Review*; James Burnham, onetime Trotskyist who now called for "rollback" of communist powers and wrote a column about the "Third World War" for the *National Review*; Frank Meyer, an ex-Communist Party activist who lived in upstate New York where he homeschooled his kids while writing and editing for the *National Review*; and Whittaker Chambers, the famous ex-communist who had exposed Alger Hiss as a spy for the Russians and who worked for the *National Review* after a stint at *Time*, sometimes sleeping with a gun beside his bed to fend off potential enemies and revenge agents sent by the Communist Party. None of these men were ready to shed "apocalyptic thinking."[3]

The 1950s was a freewheeling time for them and a time of self-definition against the flabby Eisenhower decade. Many of these thinkers stood in opposition to middle-of-the-road conservatism of the Republican Party and Ike, who, they believed, betrayed conservative ideals (indeed, some of them characterized Ike as a closet liberal). Ike was too quick to defend the postwar legacy of the New Deal, especially Social Security and labor unions, and too willing to coast on his status as a war hero rather than define himself as a leader with vision. For sure, the elderly statesman might worry about "creeping socialism," but his middle-of-the-road leadership fit the drab and conformist feel of the 1950s. Ike appeared a slumbering idiot with no sense of moral purpose, his presidency reflecting, in the words of William Buckley, a "raging national ignorance." Because many conservative intellectuals believed that "compromise with the dominant forces of this age is not possible," they learned the benefit of being free from political pressures. They could explore ideas openly. "Let the Republican Party be the Party of no philosophy, of a day-to-day pragmatism, of a guaranteed-surprise-for-the-voter-every-week." The ideas would happen elsewhere, not in the existing party structure or the thinking of political figureheads. The intellectuals would think, debate among themselves, leave politics alone, and then wait for change to happen down the road. They would rebel against their own party by holding their own conversations and would rebel against their own society by defining more clearly what it meant to be a real conservative.[4]

The 1950s became a time when defining "principles" and searching for traditions dominated the conservative mind. The decade was also a time when building a new ideology—while ideologies supposedly ended—became paramount and when conservatives started to seek out their own style that could help define the future. These were years of old ideas being put into new bottles, when those bottles were polished to appear more seductive or sometimes simply lobbed into the public as Molotov cocktails. For the conservative mind, this was a lively and engaging time of youthfulness. And so the conservative intellectual movement matched the feel of the era. Though the 1950s were known as years of conformity—when men wore gray flannel suits and drove their station wagons from their large corporate workplaces to their suburban homes where they watched television at night—it was also a time when the United States appeared to be ready for a new turn, when it seemed that inchoate rebellions would have consequences somewhere down the line. The 1950s were years marked by rebellion—rock 'n' roll, Beat writings, and the rebel style of Marlon Brando in movies. Conservatives started making their own contributions to this changing culture. It was a time, in other words, when conservative intellectuals sensed the birth of a new culture within the confines of the old.[5]

Openness bred internal dissent and bickering. The world of conservative intellectuals during the 1950s was a like a bathtub full of snapping turtles (mirroring the world of New York intellectuals and the magazine *Partisan Review* during the 1930s). All were self-assured and ready to disagree, intellectually and personally. Russell Kirk and James Burnham did not like Frank Meyer; Buckley tried to like them all. Kirk admired Buckley but thought some of his thinking about academic life narrow-minded. Chambers liked Buckley but found the young man's support for Joseph McCarthy reprehensible. Bozell and William Schlamm believed Burnham was too respectable for his own good and compromised his conservative ideas; Buckley sympathized with their view but admired Burnham too much to do anything about the matter. Some wanted conservatism to become respectable, to make a rational appeal to statesmen, and some wanted it to be rebellious and confrontational, even rude. These thinkers all cherished one another's company and played jokes on one another (sometimes, they would plaster one another's offices with pro-Ike propaganda just for laughs). And in their disagreements grew a unified and stronger conservative mind as years went on. The conservative mind would always have internal tensions, as any collective project must, but its tensions provided strength more than weakness.[6]

THE COLD WAR AS DEFINING MOMENT

Debates and disagreements helped define and eventually unify the conservative mind during the 1950s. Most important of all in creating a distinct postwar conservative mind was the Cold War. When the Soviet Union blockaded Berlin from 1948 to 1949 and China fell to communists in 1949, everything changed for conservatives. No longer was it acceptable to hold an isolationist position as it was before and during World War II when the enemy was fascism and a major ally communist. During the Cold War, the Soviet Union turned the United States not just into a world leader but the only true defender against the spread of godless communism. Western civilization faced a new crisis, either to define itself for battle or collapse under the weight of a demonic enemy. The Cold War provided a way of seeing the world in apocalyptic terms and making any idea that ideology was coming to an end untenable.[7]

To say this suggests that there is another myth haunting the Cold War period besides the "end of ideology": the myth of a "Cold War consensus," the idea that anticommunism unified Americans to such an extent that all disagreements seemed to melt away from 1950 to 1968, to the point that conservatives and liberals agreed more than they disputed. This interpretation ignores the enormous difference between the doctrine of containment—expressed in the writings of State Department planner and intellectual, George Kennan, and put into practice by President Harry Truman with the Marshall Plan and military aid to Greece and Turkey in 1947—and James Burnham's call for "liberation" and "rollback." As Burnham put it: "The policy of containment, stripped bare, is simply the bureaucratic verbalization of a policy of drift."[8] Burnham wanted to clear the deck, to do what General MacArthur had threatened to do during the Korean War—move on into China and get it back into the grips of the free world, or at least to push back on Soviet power as much as possible. Conservative intellectuals hated Eisenhower in part for his flaccid style, and that only crescendoed (ironically not for Burnham who tempered his views) when the president did not do anything to defend Hungary against Soviet expansion in 1956. When the Soviets hurled the Sputnik satellite into space, conservative intellectuals like Brent Bozell, one of Buckley's best friends at Yale and eventual brother-in-law, went berserk. Bozell blustered: "The United States now has all the rights and obligations of a man confronted with imminent and deadly assault."[9] The Cold War was more warlike than cold for conservatives.

But it was even more. Conservative intellectuals styled their responses in religious tones. They offered an alternative to the passivity and logic of containment and liberal anticommunism. Fighting would require religious certitude, battling the threat of secularism's doubts and trying to Christianize America. Around the same time that Billy Graham was taking the country by storm, a religious revival was afoot in conservative political thought. Here entered Whittaker Chambers, the godfather of the conservative mind in the postwar years. Conservatives could not help admiring the man who exposed Alger Hiss, the once respectable liberal who hobnobbed with the New Deal elite but turned out

to be a communist spy. They also loved Chambers's bestselling
and beautifully written *Witness* with its melodramatic flourish
and sad ponderings about the future of the West (but some of
that seemed too hopeless, too prone to Chambers's withdrawal
from political commitment seen throughout the later 1950s).
But what they loved the most was how Chambers's view of the
Cold War provided an understanding that emphasized values
over military strategy. Chambers, as his biographer points out,
saw the Cold War "as primarily moral and religious, rather than
military."[10] As Chambers wrote in *Witness*: "Unless the free
world, in the agony of its struggle with Communism, overcomes
its crisis by discovering, in suffering and pain, a power of faith
which will provide man's mind, at the same intensity, with the
same two certainties: a reason to live and a reason to die," the
West would fail. He went on: "If it fails, this will be the century
of the great social war. If it succeeds, this will be the century of
the great wars of faith."[11] For sure, liberals spoke of a "fighting
faith" during the Cold War, but theirs was too tentative, too rife
with the sort of complexity that constituted the enemy of the
conservative mind. As James Burnham put it: "Modern liberalism does not offer ordinary men compelling motives for personal suffering, sacrifice, and death." Conservatives offered to fill
in this absence with absolutism and religious certitude—creating
"wars of faith" in the process.[12]

It was not just Chambers and Burnham who thought this
way. Willmoore Kendall, an ex-Trotskyist who taught Buckley
a thing or two about conservative political philosophy at Yale,
argued that "no society can survive—or should survive—without
foundations driven deep in religious belief." An "open society"
could not resist an indomitable foe like communism.[13]
Understanding this meant intellectuals could not depict the Cold
War as a traditional power struggle between nations, the way
"realists" did. "Once we accept, even by indirection, the notion
that the cold war is simply an old-style power struggle," Eugene

Lyons (another ex-communist) warned, "we disarm ourselves spiritually. We strip the confrontation of precisely those ideological meanings which alone can sustain resistance to Communism inside and outside the Communist bloc."[14] There it was—the word "ideology," a term supposed to melt away into the Cold War consensus being used favorably, indeed rigorously and positively.

Extremism came easily to these conservative intellectuals who saw the Cold War in apocalyptic terms, especially considering how many of them had once subscribed to the communist doctrine themselves. To say that *National Review* was practically crawling with former communists is obvious: Max Eastman and John Dos Passos most famously and those already mentioned like Burnham, Chambers, Meyer, and Kendall. Max Eastman, the darling of the radical Left before World War I, once used a sort of "it-takes-one-to-know-one" philosophy to explain why ex-communists should lead the charge during the Cold War.[15] But Eastman ignored something here. Communism might have been ditched but certainly not the mindset that formulated its original choosing. The liberal critic and editor of *Harper's*, Bernard DeVoto, disdained the prominence ex-communists had gained in American public life during the Cold War and pointed out that "embracing communism, like religious conversion, is an act of the total personality." (Chambers confirmed the point when he described that he entered the Communist Party "with somewhat the same feeling with which another man might enter a religious order.")[16] DeVoto believed readers were right to question a man's judgment who had admitted abject error in the past and who still held out hope for absolute choices, because extremism still structured the new position espoused. When Arthur Schlesinger Jr. called James Burnham a "man in a permanent apocalypsis," he meant that Burnham moved too easily from a Marxist theory of capitalism's inevitable collapse during the 1930s to a fear that containment would lead to the inevitable collapse of Western civilization during the 1950s.[17]

Schlesinger was onto something. Former communists could not leave behind their extremism; they were too infatuated with it because it ordered the world they observed. This stylistic element in the conservative mind is crucial to understand. In one of the best depictions of Whittaker Chambers, Lionel Trilling's fictional account of Gifford Maxim in *The Middle of the Journey*, we hear a character complain: "I somehow don't quite like his relation to his ideas."[18] The reaction was against not just the "reactionary" ideas held but against the style and tone of those ideas and how quickly they had replaced an earlier fanaticism. There is no better statement to describe a mind that is in constant search for absolutes and for a totalizing view of the world that could wrap up every detail into a coherent philosophy. Chambers and others on the Right replaced the theology of communism with a theology of conservatism. The style remained unchanged.[19]

Extremism also helps explain why references to war litter conservative writing during these years. As James Burnham argued, war is a constitutive part of the conservative view of the world: "Wars are not accidents in history, but integral and even normal parts of the process of history." Absolutism—a faith that one's ideas possess objective truth—helped justify doing anything necessary to ensure those ideas their rightful victory, which meant doing things that could be destructive to the original principles themselves. It meant that relativistic means could be adopted, because the ends were so absolute in their rightness (this would lay the ground for the postmodern conservatism to come later, as we will see). Destruction and the politics of attack—not things that would seem very conservative by first appearance—were justified. Politics, for the conservative mind during the Cold War, became a hunt for an enemy. War became a logical extension of this disposition.[20]

Extremism provided another root of the postwar conservative mind: the tendency to cleanse and purge. Extremism faced off against extremism. Ex-communist conservatives crossed the Rubicon armed with the sectarian tactics from their past. For instance, Whittaker Chambers famously deposed Ayn Rand from the conservative movement because she was too materialistic and had rejected religious faith. Rand (no ex-communist) was certainly apocalyptic and absolutist in her thought; she had laid out in her fiction what she would later call the "virtue of self-ishness," a hard and absolutist libertarian philosophy for the Right. Reviewing her book *Atlas Shrugged*, Chambers asserted Rand was a bad writer prone to exaggeration and an elitist with a "dictatorial tone."[21] She was too materialistic and logocentric (a term that will come later in this story) for the conservative movement, and Buckley unleashed Chambers on her like an attack dog, expecting the dynamite of extremism to ignite. Readers of the *National Review* deemed the review controversial and wrote to complain. One compared Chambers's attack to the "methods" employed by the *Daily Worker* against those who did not follow the Communist Party line. But another sided with Chambers. He explained that "only when the ideological perverts are removed from the camp, will true (ergo Christian) conservatism make the gains which are imperative for the survival of our way of life." Chambers made one thing clear: the conservative mind could never be simply libertarian (though it would incorporate that outlook as part of its scaffolding). The conservative mind needed religion too, in order to provide an ideal form of certitude ready for battle.[22]

More telling was the purge of Peter Viereck. Viereck had written one of the first postwar reassessments of the conservative mind, *Conservatism Revisited* (1949). He imagined a respectable conservatism and discussed its necessary "aristocratic spirit" and sense of "proportion and measure," "self-restraint," and "continuity." But in the same breath, he called for the United States to support social democrats in Europe as the only bulwark against the spread of communism (suggesting flexibility with economic and political principles when it came to looking at a world in crisis). As the 1950s proceeded, Viereck believed conservatives needed to ally with liberals, searching for a centrist politics that could pull America through the Cold War. He cited a "non-party philosophy close to that of Adlai Stevenson among Democrats, Clifford Case [a centrist politician from New Jersey] among Republicans." This sort of compromise was too much for Frank Meyer. Meyer saw Viereck as a man with "unexceptionably Liberal sentiments," a conservative poser. It was time to purge fake conservatives. To compromise with them was to surrender too much of what should be core to the conservative identity.[23]

Lurking behind the charge of pseudoconservatism, of course, was the *real* enemy that all conservatives had united against by the postwar period: modern liberalism. When Chambers started to see communists having infiltrated the New Deal apparatus, he started to believe that liberalism and communism were Siamese twins. There were of course actual communists in the New Deal apparatus, but Chambers extended this point to paint a picture of ideologies blending into one another. There was "common cause" between communism and liberalism and the "New Deal" was "only superficially a reform movement" and really a "genuine revolution" that had changed "power relationships within the nation" in order to empower government over business. Conservatives hoped to split the world down the middle by suggesting that liberalism shared so much with communism that the only true divide was between communism and conservatism. As William Rusher, who became publisher of *National Review* in 1957, put it: "The Liberal Establishment shares Communism's materialist principles." It was another step, but not too far, for James Burnham to write a few years later that "liberalism is the ideology of

Western suicide." Chambers, Rusher, and Burnham, in their own statements, had charted the future of the conservative mind. "*Boobus Liberalis*" was now a permanent target in its sight—not just permanent but even constitutive in the conservative mind. Without it, the conservative mind threatened to become homeless and unharbored.[24]

In the Beginning, There Was Buckley: On the Original Split Personality of the Right

Leading the battle during the Cold War first and foremost was William F. Buckley. All histories of conservative ideas tell how Buckley held the movement together. But he held it together, in large part, by ingesting different styles of conservative opposition to liberalism. Through him and his founding of the *National Review*, these strains resolved themselves. The conservative style became one of a permanent rebel bucking the liberal establishment.

Buckley's biography screams out elitism. He appeared the closest thing to Peter Viereck's "aristocratic spirit," at least the closest thing America could produce. Born into a wealthy family (its money made from oil), Buckley grew up on a "forty-seven-acre estate" in Sharon, Connecticut. He rode horses and sailed; his life was populated with "cooks and maids." He cultivated a sense of "hauteur" at an early age. In college, he was described—and this by someone who actually liked him—as an "arrogant guy." When he grew up, he learned to speak in tones remarkably aristocratic, arching his eyebrows, pulling his head back, and then saying something that sounded almost British in its accent.[25]

And yet Buckley was also an outsider—a Catholic and Irishman in predominantly WASP Connecticut. That became clearer when he attended Yale University from 1946 to 1950, after serving in World War II. As it did for many young men, college encouraged Buckley to rebel and honed what his biographer John Judis called a "defiance of authority." Most students at Yale voted straight-Republican, so Buckley reserved his venom for his professors, whom he believed taught atheism and Keynesianism. He wanted to fight back against them, so he developed the necessary skills. He joined Yale's debating team (he was thought to be excellent) and wrote opinion editorials for the *Yale Daily News*. He even had the chance to write an Alumni Day speech right before his graduation, in which he planned to flay the university for not firing certain faculty (it was seen as too controversial and thus never given).[26]

Buckley's plan to pillory Yale was then turned into his first book, *God and Man at Yale* (1951), a foundational text for the postwar conservative mind. It had a straightforward argument: Yale should dismiss professors who taught ideas in opposition to conservative principles. The bulk of the book showed Buckley pouring through lecture notes, textbooks, and course catalogs in order to prove how collectivism in economics and atheism in religious matters were ubiquitous at Yale. Buckley's penchant for controversy shined in his program for action. This recent graduate was pointing his finger at the administrators of Yale; he railed at them, saying they were not doing their job. They were not following the orders of "trustees" and the "alumni" who "are committed to the desirability of fostering both a belief in God, and a recognition of the merits of our economic system."[27] Those people at the helm, charged with the highest ethical responsibility of educating the young, were too enamored with "academic freedom," a concept Buckley quickly dismissed as a superstition. The concept of academic freedom had whittled down teaching to mere "professional competence." It thereby devalued the importance of "character" (142) and the commitment of a professor to conservative principles. After all, professors were merely the "intermediaries" of the president, those who delivered the beliefs of the trustees and alums to the students (172). "Professors" who did not perform the task of the intermediary "should be discharged," Buckley concluded (197).

The message of the book and its knowing style worked in tandem. The young rebel Buckley assessed his condemnation of Yale's administration well when he wrote: "I have some notion of the bitter opposition that this book will inspire" (xvi). But he shrugged off the reaction; conservatives *had to become* controversial, even disruptive of the ordinary operations of academe, if they were to accomplish anything. This was time for battle, not for relaxing and toking up a cigar or mixing a martini, the way other alums might. And Buckley concluded that he and his small cadre of conservative colleagues were the vanguard for change. "The conservatives, as a minority, are the new radicals. The evidence is overwhelming" (107).

Buckley *had* learned from one of his professors at Yale, namely, Wilmoore Kendall, who provided the book with its oddly populist hues. Of course, it is counterintuitive to think a defense of wealthy graduates of Yale could take on populist hues. But as Buckley's biographer points out, the young dissenter had applied "Kendall's populist majoritarianism to Yale" by suggesting that "the alumni were both the rightful majority and the repository of conservative wisdom."[28] This was no populism of pitchfork-carrying farmers. It was a populism of wealthy men telling those trained into scholarship—purported experts but really little more than moral functionaries—how to run the ship, an anti-intellectualism on the march for the upper classes. Indeed, Bruce Barton, the advertising maven who hated the New Deal more than anyone and who agreed that things were awry at Yale, looked at Buckley's solution to the problem with bewilderment. "Letting the alumni dictate the teaching, what could be more terrifying? Are these noisy perennial sophomores, who dress up in silly costumes and get drunk at reunions, who spend their thousands of dollars buying halfbacks and quarterbacks, and following the Big Blue Team—are they to be the nation's mental mentors?"[29] That might sound like little more than a humorous put-down, but it was a serious point and cut to the chase.

Buckley was suggesting that "professional competence" and scholarly training mattered little if citizens, in this case wealthy alums, were upset with what was being taught at *their* university. This point became a foundation for future conservative thought.[30]

The book was a sensation. It crystallized Buckley's profile as a rebel. It even won him friends from the Left. Dwight Macdonald, a Trotskyist turned crotchety cultural critic, championed Buckley's style. Buckley was someone who would "rather argue than eat, a trait I find endearing. Had he been born a generation earlier, he would have been making the cafeterias of 14th Street ring with Marxian dialectics." He liked that Buckley seemed "brisk, brash, indecorous." Those were good characteristics for the caustic Macdonald. And he liked that Buckley played an "old familiar script" so well: "Campus Rebel Flays Faculty." It was not just the Left though who saw it this way. As historian Gregory Schneider points out, the book became "to young conservatives during the 1950s" what "C. Wright Mills's *The Power Elite* and Paul Goodman's *Growing Up Absurd* were for left-wing students." Mills was the motorcycle-riding rebel whose ideas helped inform a nascent New Left and Goodman the anarchist bisexual: Buckley was somehow their implausible equivalent.[31]

It should be pointed out here that Buckley's *God and Man at Yale* appeared five years before *The Power Elite* and almost a full ten before *Growing Up Absurd*. In other words, Buckley was *pioneering* a style that would change American culture throughout the 1950s. The style of the rebel in existential revolt against a conformist society that armored itself against criticism—no one can understand 1950s America without this concept as a guide.[32] The decade would become known for conformity and complacency, but it was also a time known for pugnacious young men whose disaffection became a hot commodity. There was James Dean, the cool and detached young man who lived his life fast both in the movies and reality. There was Marlon Brando with his "lonely eyes, the scornful lip, the inarticulate mumblings, and the controlled rage that made being 'cool' the strategy of survival."[33] There were young kids wearing leather jackets and listening to rock 'n' roll. There was *Mad* magazine (started in 1952) and, of course, the Beat writers like Jack Kerouac (whom Buckley and Chambers actually admired) and poet Allen Ginsberg. Buckley cornered a market in the culture of rebellion. He was the young Turk taking it to the bureaucratic man who ran the university. He knew how to be a sensation—an *enfant terrible*—that sold an image of angry young men whose market value would continue to grow as the decade proceeded.

If Buckley's style of rebellion against liberal bureaucracy provided a legacy that still lives today, the message of *God and Man at Yale* itself became an enduring part of the conservative mind from that point onward. Writing for Yale's student newspaper, Buckley had called for "student opinion of teachers" to play a larger role in faculty evaluation. The student, after all, was a consumer who had the right to determine the quality of the product—in this case, classroom content. Buckley made this explicit in *God and Man at Yale*, where he pointed out that the "long haired professor" had his research "in large part subsidized by the consumers of teaching." Consumer satisfaction, Buckley seemed to suggest, should be measured and given influence. As M. Stanton Evans, a young conservative journalist out of the Midwest, put it, Buckley's book helped alert "students to the bias in some of the course materials" and showed "that the canons of 'academic freedom' were being only partially observed in New Haven." To use a term now in fashion on the Left, Buckley was *empowering* conservative students.[34]

Buckley knew he was onto something and never let up on the book's central theme, long after it hit the remainder tables. His column at the *National Review* would take as its title "The Ivory Tower." Academe was starting to play a central role in research and development necessary for the Cold War, and more

and more students were flocking to colleges as a result of the
GI benefits. So higher education was a smart target. Buckley
foresaw the culture wars of our own period and made academe
central to the conservative mind—winning it a permanent place
in the conservative pantheon of enemies. Buckley himself would
continue the war personally throughout the 1950s. For instance,
he would call for the detenuring of Arthur Schlesinger Jr., who
had "put history at the disposal of ideology." The choice of target was telling: Schlesinger, after all, was a devoted anticommunist who had received high praise for his popular history books.
That did not matter to Buckley. Because this so-called scholar
wrote "a perversion of" real history, why did he deserve a
"Harvard chair"? Of course, Harvard was too far gone for
Buckley (it had always been Yale's liberal twin). But Buckley's
point was the gibe itself—the taking down of a respected historian who won big-name prizes and a respected institution that
had enormous prestige. In his small war against Yale and Harvard,
Buckley was charging up conservative students for future battle.
In so many words, he was mapping out a future culture war.[35]

There was a problem though. Where was the agency for
change in all of this? *God and Man at Yale*, after all, was a book
lacking heroes. The professors and administrators were bankrupt;
the students appeared victims; the only ones mounting the bar-
ricades were Buckley and his fellow radical conservatives (and
they were a minority). In his next book, Buckley created a hero
of sorts or at least a change agent—a man who was fighting a
noble and misunderstood battle. That man was Senator Joseph
McCarthy, who was starting his ascendance to newfound star-
dom as a conservative anticommunist. The senator, around the
time that *God and Man and Yale* was still being discussed, claimed
that he had a "list of names" of known communists "made
known to the Secretary of State and who nevertheless are still
working and shaping the policy of the State Department."[36]
Soon thereafter McCarthy reached the height of his power by

pursuing investigations of communist influence as chair of the Government Operations Committee. Never did he unearth any communists not already known about, but the senator certainly continued to wage a one-man war against the idea that communists occupied the highest echelons of American power.

Buckley championed the senator's controversial activism by cowriting *McCarthy and His Enemies* in 1954 with his old debating team friend, Brent Bozell. By all accounts, the book lacked the pizzazz of Buckley's first. It read like a legal brief or "a courtroom document," plodding its way through case after case, often getting lost in details. McCarthy was a difficult hero, and Buckley had to admit his champion's faults and propensity toward exaggeration. The book hedged its bets often, arguing that, no, McCarthy did not really introduce any new communist agents at the Tydings Committee, as promised, he just raised suspicions about the effectiveness of Truman's Loyalty Act and how the State Department applied it. Often, the book offered a "McCarthy-is-no-worse-than-any-other-person" type of defense, which was not exactly a ringing endorsement. "Our Liberal statesmen, journalists, professors, and preachers ululate whenever the hyperbole is used against them" as it was by McCarthy, Buckley and Bozell wrote in their strange and pretentious style. "But in their mouths, it becomes a righteous weapon with which to smite down the Philistines." In other words, McCarthy was just doing what the other side did.[37]

Whittaker Chambers chafed at Buckley's choice of hero. McCarthy for him had a "flair for the sensational" and was "a rabble rouser and a slugger."[38] Chambers's protest might help explain Buckley's original fascination with the senator. To a certain extent, McCarthy's style fit Buckley's. Bozell would later praise McCarthy for his "buoyancy, strength of will, awesome singlemindedness." That last term said it all: what was admirable in McCarthy was his obsessive zeal.[39] Besides, Buckley did not want to defend McCarthy's specific charges but rather to praise him for the "enemies" he made, as the book title suggested. Buckley and Bozell consistently aligned McCarthy against the "intelligentsia" who condemned him. These liberal windbags, it was pointed out, talked of a "reign of terror as the result of the activities of Senator McCarthy." Of course, this for them was nonsense, as liberals dominated just about every institution of American political culture (the press and the media foremost). And if McCarthy was doing a good job at angering the liberal intelligentsia, then conservative writers must toss out his bad side and make McCarthy an ally, a fellow rebel with a cause. Buckley sought and got McCarthy's help with the book (though the senator was too deep into drink at the time to do much).[40]

Buckley hoped other conservative intellectuals would flock to his newfound hero, even if Chambers refused. Conservatives, he suggested, needed to take sides in battles, even when such choices made them uncomfortable. A high-minded, aristocratic battle against communism was not going to take place any time soon; conservatives had to settle for what they had at hand—in this case, the tough-ass style of a pugnacious, heavy-drinking senator coming out of the democratic Midwest. Faith in the cause and its necessary ends required alliances that were not always that clean, tidy, or perfect. McCarthy got his support from the masses, winning election hands-down after his famous Wheeling speech (and talking up his attacks on privileged members of the State Department). As historian John Patrick Diggins once quipped: "Only in America do conservative elites turn to the democratic masses for popular support against non-conforming liberals."[41]

Buckley was largely successful. The *National Review* would continue to support McCarthy as late as 1957, praising his ability to "fire the Western will."[42] Supporting McCarthy helped nurture the more important task at hand—attacking liberalism as soft and showing the rebellious feel of the postwar conservative mind. Frank Meyer argued, in a way that would foreshadow a postmodernist turn taken later, that McCarthy's tactics were the "small change of American politics—nothing that has not been used on every side of every political controversy for scores of years." Absolute principles and tactical relativism wedded themselves within the synapses of the conservative mind. Liberals hated McCarthy because he accused their creed as complicit with communism and because he seemed fanatical in his attack. McCarthy showed the "integral characteristics of the Liberalism which" became "increasingly predominant" and that make clear how "our present leadership can neither resist the infiltration of Communists within nor concert an effective strategy against Communists without." Meyer built on Chambers's argument that the New Deal bled into socialism—what Meyer himself termed the "socialist equivalence of the aims of the Liberals and the Communists." McCarthy had shown how liberalism gave birth to communism, and that's why liberals attacked him. Fear and hypocrisy fired the liberal attack on McCarthy.[43]

William Schlamm, another ex-Communist who wrote the "prologue" to *McCarthy and His Enemies*, especially hated how the media ganged up on McCarthy after his fall from grace and his censure in the Senate in 1954. Schlamm characterized McCarthy as innocent and naive, the press as demonic. He especially hated the lawyer Joseph Welch, who attacked McCarthy at the famous Army-McCarthy hearings in 1954. Welch had become a hero to some, his words "Senator, have you no sense of decency?" living long after he originally said them. But for Schlamm, Welch was little more than a slick-talking fool who fit an age "ruled by the soft-spoken and the soft-brained, the well-mannered and the lukewarm, the genteel and half-educated asses." "We, too, have seen the gargoyles stare and sneer at us," Schlamm went on, explaining how conservatives had grown used to being attacked in the media and by the liberal elite and how he thought of himself as rebel. "We, too, are reaching out to crush them. We mean it. We are McCarthyites." So here it was: a sense of absolutist faith melding into a call to do what needed to be done and choosing heroes who could never be seen as angels but as tactical agents of change and who could play to the populist and antielitist tones of America's political culture.[44]

McCarthy went down to censure just as Bozell and Buckley's book came out. Add to this that in the three years since *God and Man at Yale* was published, the university had not fired any teachers, and it would seem Buckley's personal campaigns had failed from his college years through 1954. The "liberal establishment"—a term that would become popular around this time—had stood strong. Buckley might have thrown rocks at the liberal establishment, but they glanced off its edifice. Still, he had accomplished more than first appears. Even before founding the *National Review*, he had unleashed two themes for the conservative mind to build on: a rebel populism (zinging Yale and supporting McCarthy) and an older aristocratic style. It was the rebel populist style that would win out. This was not the conservatism of an Edmund Burke or Joseph de Maistre, that is, an aristocratic defense of a social hierarchy. But it promised real enemies (academe and liberals) and real heroes (McCarthy). It also promised a hearing in the United States—a country that would never come to appreciate the sort of aristocratic and Burkean conservatism Buckley might have secretly pined for but one that could admire Dean's or Brando's toughness. To do battle, certain things had to be accepted, including America's cruder and tougher political landscape.

THE *NATIONAL REVIEW* AND THE ANTI-INTELLECTUALISM OF RIGHT-WING INTELLECTUALS

By 1954, Buckley had two books under his belt. That's pretty good for a young man about to turn thirty. He had a celebrity status to boot. Nonetheless, he wanted more. Irving Howe, who founded the left-wing magazine *Dissent* in 1954, once stated: "When intellectuals can do nothing else, they start a magazine." Buckley might have said the same thing at just the same time. As he looked at the Republican Party and Ike's leadership, he decided it was time to found his own magazine, and the *National Review* became his greatest lifetime accomplishment. Before it began in 1955, there were two serious magazines of the Right: the *Freeman*, which was ultimately too libertarian to become a big tent for conservative thought, and the *American Mercury*, which was too isolationist and cranky to have a wider appeal. There was also the weekly *Human Events*, but the articles there were too short to nurture a deeper intellectual style (and it too was isolationist). So when *National Review* hit newsstands, its importance could not be overlooked. It brought together all the different elements of the conservative mind—libertarianism, religion, and aggressive foreign policy—under one roof.[45]

Buckley's split personality—between an aristocratic demeanor and a rebel style—played itself out in the magazine's pages. Its founding statements ran mostly to the side of the rebellious, though still with a residual Burkean tinge. *National Review* would "forthrightly oppose the prevailing trend of public opinion" and thumb its nose at the " 'respectable' press." There was nothing good about the "middle of the road." After all, the *National Review* had to be authentic and embody "personal journalism," which meant "the manly presentation of deeply felt convictions" and an embrace of "controversy." One thing for sure, the magazine would not be a "jaded defense of the status quo." These were radicals after all, or "non-licensed non-conformists" in Buckley's own words. That is why the magazine offered the "hottest game in town." But then, in the next breath, Buckley described his magazine as standing "athwart history, yelling Stop" against the winds of progress. This was the very little bit of Burke and Southern Agrarianism, merely a rhetorical gloss, that could still couch itself in a predominantly rebellious and forward-looking call to arms.[46]

As John Chamberlain, ex-socialist now turned conservative, noted, *National Review* smashed the stereotype of the conservative as fuddy-duddy. After all, he argued, "the radical zest has passed from the Liberals and found a new home across the lines."[47] One reader concurred when she wrote in to the *National Review* to encourage its "youthfulness of spirit."[48] An editor like James Burnham might chafe at such a spirit with his sophisticated "professorial" style, as might Chambers, who always held to a sophisticated intellectualism, even while his ideas helped justify a more radical conservatism.[49] But their style gave way to the magazine's young, pugnacious, and hip tones. Editors would purge fake conservatives, for sure, but they would also recruit young writers whose politics did not fit the conservative mold. In the search for young blood, William Buckley wound up hiring John Leonard (who eventually moved to the left-wing *Nation*), Garry Wills (a conservative at the time whose politics would eventually scatter all over the place), and Joan Didion (whose western childhood nurtured a libertarian streak but whose politics evaded easy categorization). Leonard believed Buckley hired these young writers for their "zippy lip," figuring that he would "take care of our politics with the charismatic science of his own personality."[50] Youthfulness and zesty writing mattered as much as conservative principles. And thus, the sociologist and New York intellectual Nathan Glazer could refer, in the 1960s, to the "hip conservatism of the *National Review*" without giving the comment second thought.[51]

Style mattered, as it allowed conservatives to reach out beyond their self-perceived marginality. Buckley believed his magazine would aim "at thoughtful people, at opinion makers. We feel that before it is possible to bring the entire nation around politically, we have got to engage the attention of people who for a long time have felt that the conservative position is moribund."[52] This grandiose aim was more a problem than first might appear. Conservatives, after all, had traditionally distrusted intellectuals, who seemed necessarily wedded to the project of the Enlightenment. As Edmund Burke once complained, modern intellectuals "have no respect for the wisdom of others, but they pay it off by a very full measure of confidence in their own."[53] Following this line of reasoning, Whittaker Chambers once derided the "poisonous puddle of the intellectuals."[54] Russell Kirk believed the intellectual often held "a ridiculous contempt for everything in heaven and earth but his own notion."[55] Intellectuals—the heroes of Ayn Rand, who was now being blasted out of the movement—were so pledged to rationalism that they destroyed the "higher reason which grows out of a respect for the wisdom of our ancestors and out of the endeavor to apprehend that transcendent order which gives us our nature."[56] The modern intellectual was part of the problem. But the *National Review*, paradoxically, directed its message at modern intellectuals dissatisfied with liberalism. A conundrum indeed. The conservative mind was obviously intellectual by definition, but it had to blast intellectuals as pompous and elitist at the same time. It was a new anti-intellectualism of the intellectuals.[57]

Conservative anti-intellectualism played well in 1950s America. After all, the conservative critique of the modern intellectual provided one basis for derisive talk about "eggheads" that spread throughout the early years of the decade. One conservative author, writing in 1952, had defined the "egghead" as "supercilious and surfeited with conceit and contempt for the experience of more sound and able men" and prone to liberal desires or what he labeled "bleeding heart" tendencies. President Eisenhower joked about intellectuals, saying at a press conference that he had "heard a definition of an intellectual that I thought was very interesting: a man who takes more words than are necessary to tell more than he knows."[58] "Anti-intellectualism," the umbrella term under which historian Richard Hofstadter famously yoked these statements, was always a strong current in the American past and became central to 1950s culture, as did the icon of the youthful rebel (and in some cases these two cultural tendencies went hand in hand, such as when Norman Mailer praised the "hipster" who rebelled against conformity and rational thought at the same time).[59]

Could conservatives be intellectuals if so disturbed by the modern Enlightenment and rationality? Kirk—after blasting intellectuals—went on to lay out an alternative model for the "conservative mind." He believed the conservative intellectual had to search the past for a usable tradition of ideas. The intellectual tradition he presented in *The Conservative Mind* was rather quirky; after all, it had to hold ideas while not trusting logic and rationality too much. Kirk's own history of ideas zoomed all over the place (to the United States, then Europe, then back) and threw a wide net, at times becoming muddled and incoherent. There was Edmund Burke, John Adams, Alexis de Tocqueville, Disraeli, and Nathaniel Hawthorne. The tradition included Federalists who championed national unity over decentralization and southerners who championed states rights and local government over national unity. This was, in other words, a hodge-podge tradition with a whiff of elitism. Kirk openly bemoaned universal suffrage and defined "modern public opinion" as a "fumbling creature hungry for something to satisfy the craving engendered by his nominal literacy." He warned that "American character, individualistic, covetous, contemptuous of restraint, always had been stubborn clay for the keepers of tradition to mould into civilization."[60]

Then when he tried to popularize the ideas a year later in his *A Program for Conservatives*, he toned down his elitism and explained how one of his fellow conservatives was a "truck driver." He could assert, without necessarily developing the point, that "our native radical movements, like Populism, commonly have been inspired, however curiously, by certain conservative instincts." Populist rebels seemed more appealing than the aristocratic defenses written by Edmund Burke. And Kirk could play up the idea that eggheads and intellectuals were out of touch with ordinary people and therefore victims of their own "consummate snobbery." He appeared simultaneously an elitist intellectual who distrusted the masses and a radical democrat who championed populism. This was a model for the conservative mind, even if it caused dissonance through the years.[61]

Kirk was not alone in presenting this tension in conservative social thought. Though the *National Review* would aim to convert writers, thinkers, and opinion makers, Buckley would continue to expound the central themes of *God and Man at Yale*—his disdain for the professoriate's attack on religion and a sense that intellectuals were predispositioned toward disobeying conservative principles. And it is easy to see why: conservatives were now identifying intellectualism with their major foe—liberalism. The word "intellectual" was becoming fast interchangeable with the term "liberal." Kirk had already learned this idea from one of his and Buckley's intellectual heroes, Richard Weaver. The southern critic Weaver had equated liberalism and intellectuality. It was not difficult. He pointed out that liberals refused to take sides. They were, in simpler terms, wishy-washy. There was a "propensity to moral and intellectual flabbiness on the part of the Liberal." And this was also a feature of the egghead, the thinker who always saw the other side of an argument instead of choosing what was right. A "non-committal attitude" defined liberalism. Thus, in opposing liberalism, conservatives aimed their ire at intellectuals as well, even as they might try to win them over. They envisioned conservatives not as effete intellectuals but as tough-asses, warriors armed with certitude. Conservatives were deciders, not equivocators. This ideal allowed the conservative mind to play well in America—a country that seemed distrustful of the life of the mind.[62]

LOOKING FOR TRADITION AND AGENCY
IN ALL THE WRONG PLACES: FROM
SOUTHERN AGRARIANISM TO
SOUTHERN STRATEGY

Conservatives knew criticizing was not enough. They needed to offer an alternative to liberalism. That explains William Buckley's celebration of McCarthy against his enemies, Chambers's call for religious certitude in fighting the Cold War, and James Burnham's theory of "rollback." It also explains the fascination conservatives showed in all things southern. Take Russell Kirk for instance. Though a northerner by birth, he did graduate studies at Duke University (1940–1941) and, from that moment onward, saw the South as a region that offered an alternative to the liberal, individualistic, and industrialized North. Much of the conservative intellectual tradition he championed was southern. In *The Conservative Mind*, he tried to "keep clear of that partisan controversy over slavery" to plumb the real meaning of the South. He had already written *Randolph of Roanoke* (1951) to offer a glimpse of "old Republican political thought" with an emphasis on property rights, a traditionalist obligation of the individual for society, and a "defense of the states against federal encroachment." John Calhoun inherited these ideas and pushed them toward a theory of nullification and concurrent majority, all couched within a broader defense of the southern way of life. To be taken seriously, Kirk believed, the conservative mind had to pay homage to its southern roots.[63]

More important in this area of social thought than Kirk was Richard Weaver. He had grown up in Lexington, Kentucky, and had embraced socialism at an early age. Attending Vanderbilt University, he shed his youthful socialism as he fell in love with the writings of the Southern Agrarians. After graduating, he moved north to teach at the University of Chicago in 1944, where he remained until his death in 1963. During his Chicago years, he wrote about and pined away for his southern homeland.

And to no surprise, Weaver signed up with the *National Review* from the beginning.[64]

Weaver knew, better than anyone, that there was a pre–World War II legacy for the postwar conservative mind to build on: the philosophical writings of the Southern Agrarians who saw in their region an indigenous source of conservative values (briefly discussed in the introduction to this book). The authors of *I'll Take My Stand* (1930), who called themselves the "Twelve Southerners," expounded on their region's agrarian way of life and explained why it provided an alternative to the rapidly modernizing North. The South had resisted the "gospel of Progress." It saw the natural world as "mysterious and contingent" and thus treated it with awe and respect, rather than as a commodity to be used (as was the case up North). The region's small farms and large plantations nurtured a simpler life, more in tune with the seasons and natural labor patterns. The South cultivated respect for tradition and was more religious than the North. And as far as the South's race relations, Robert Penn Warren (writing as one of the Twelve Southerners) explained, they were harmonious, if not based on equality. Overall, the South built stable, organic social relations.[65]

The authors of this book became Weaver's lifelong teachers. But as much as Weaver was a southerner, he was also a philosopher in search of truth with a capital T. He became famous for his critique of "nominalism," a doctrine "which denies that universals have a real existence." In *Ideas Have Consequences* (1948), a classic of postwar conservative thought (much like Buckley's *God and Man at Yale*), Weaver upheld universal and objective values against modernity's relativistic assault. Like philosophers in the German tradition of idealism, Weaver feared that nominalism had "banish[ed] the reality which is perceived by the intellect" and left modern humans only with "the senses." He placed a sharp divide between "the material and the transcendental." Weaver's position was shared by many conservatives who abhorred relativism, especially the sort found in John Dewey's educational ideas about learning by doing (that is, pragmatism)—a scourge of the conservative mind.[66]

But Weaver's subsequent writings posed a strange contradiction: as much as he upheld universal objective values untainted by empiricism or the "senses," he still wound up tying these values to a concrete historical place—the American South—thus making them sound historically contingent. Reading Weaver was, at times, like reading G.W.F. Hegel, who argued that universal reason had unfurled itself in his own dear Prussia. In *Ideas Have Consequences*, Weaver flew back and forth from expounding philosophical objectivism to championing the historical ideal of the gentleman in the South. Then later, he would argue that the South (a "regime") challenged "liberalism" directly. The South's aristocratic features and its sense of "transcendence, which has been referred to seriously as its religiousness and scornfully as its Bible Beltism" could pose an alternative to the "anomie" of modernity and liberalism.[67] His conservatism teetered between philosophical absolutism and a search for historical examples as carriers of its principles. Ironically, he did not learn from the leading Southern Agrarian poet and critic Allen Tate who warned that his colleagues might have, by emphasizing the southern tradition, "confounded secular and sacred history."[68]

The tension between universalism and historicism did not stop here but worked its way throughout the conservative mind. First and most obviously, the southern tradition, with its emphasis on religion, traditionalism, and agrarianism, did not necessarily work in synch with free-market capitalism. Weaver himself railed against finance capital and profligate wealth. But this only pointed to the almost mythical sense of the South that Weaver clung to. After all, the South had done plenty of good cash business with the North before the Civil War and then raced forward, after Reconstruction, to industrialize as quickly as possible.

By the time that Weaver wrote, the South was, in the words of one economic historian, a "low wage region in a high wage country," doing plenty of industrial work. The region was no more critical of capitalism than the bankers and financiers castigated by Weaver.[69]

The real tension the South provided for the conservative mind could be found in its bifurcated political culture. The region, before and after the Civil War, was split down the middle— between, on the one hand, a love of "chivalry" and honor among the upper classes and, on the other, a yeoman populism that often resented wealth and cultivation, a split, to put it crudely, between a love for organic social order and radical egalitarianism. The South's religion could be seen as a source of stability or radical energy exhibited in revivals, itinerant preachers, and tent meetings. Conservative intellectuals like Weaver might depict the South as a land of gentlemanly chivalry, but there was another side to it. Consider W. J. Cash, whose *The Mind of the South* (1941) came out seven years before *Ideas Have Consequences*. Cash, who had also grown up in the South, wrote about chivalry and the gentlemanly tradition, for sure, but he also discussed a "spontaneous" element in the South exhibited in such things as "raw whisky" and "wild yells" in the "backwoods" and an age-old tradition of mobs and lynchings.[70]

Weaver, too, knew of this populist side and, after he passed away, Willmoore Kendall argued that Weaver had died a populist.[71] Weaver's populism clashed with his own praise for the southern gentleman ideal. The two sides of the South lived in Weaver's own mind. But the populist side—and a particular variant of it—would become more pronounced as the South's history changed during the postwar years. After all, the Southern Agrarians, from whom Weaver learned so much, might have been able to depict the South as a land of racial and social harmony, but conservatives during World War II and the years following witnessed the birth of the modern civil rights movement.

A. Philip Randolph's threat to hold a March on Washington to protest racial discrimination during the war built up steam and culminated in the *Brown v. Board of Education* decision in 1954, the Montgomery bus boycott that quickly followed in 1955, and then Martin Luther King Jr.'s rise to leadership over a national movement. The southern populist tradition was fast becoming a defense not just of white supremacy but also of a grassroots democracy that resulted in what has been called "massive resistance"—the South's populist, aggressive defense of its laws and social practices against the demands of the civil rights movement.[72]

Richard Weaver knew the circumstances in his homeland were rapidly changing. And he did not remain silent. If anything, apocalypse took hold, displacing talk of gentility and social order. He intentionally blurred the line between liberalism and communism to suggest that communism was behind much of the civil rights movement. Communism, after all, promoted "racial mingling." The Supreme Court was the "'running dog' of the Kremlin." And just in case he was not being clear enough, he explained:"'Integration' and 'Communization' are, after all, pretty closely synonymous. In light of what is happening today, the first may be little more than a euphemism for the second." Communism promised to create a mass society devoid of difference, and the civil rights movement was doing its work down South.[73] America was in danger of taking Lincoln's "house divided" speech too seriously and imposing an authoritarian nationalism from above.[74]

Weaver was not alone in this. Events kept boiling up to press on the conservative mind during the late 1950s. In 1957, the Little Rock crisis erupted, with Arkansas Governor Orval Faubus refusing to open public schools to black students and white mobs mounting to back up his resistance and face down National Guard troops. The *National Review* argued that the Supreme Court had "illegalized a whole set of deeply-rooted folkways." The resulting mob violence should come as no surprise. After all, the South was asserting the states' rights doctrine in bold and new ways. The mob violence drew from the teachings of conservative political philosophy. Because "liberalism rejects custom, revelation, and tradition" and imposes "reason," it is no surprise to find battles in the streets over civil rights, writers at the *National Review* concluded. "The cult of reason divorced from tradition and faith ends in the brute appeal to force." Hence, the National Guard's bayonets were a logical extension of liberalism, and they had created a new set of rebels ready for action and maybe even war. The editors cited favorably Mississippi novelist and modernist hero William Faulkner's statement that he would "fight for Mississippi against the United States even if it meant going out into the street and shooting Negroes." Ironically, Faulkner had been suggesting a "go slow" approach to integration, as the slogan became known throughout the South, not a stance of "do not go at all," which is what *National Review* seemed to suggest.[75]

States' rights as a political concept justified the "massive resistance" of the South—the right, as John Calhoun would have seen it, to place some source of power between the lone individual and the federal government. But it is also irrefutable that racism played a role here. In discussing the Senate defeat of the 1957 Civil Rights Bill, the editors were cheerful about the impact of a potential move toward civil disobedience on the part of whites and were willing to back their claims in sheer power politics. Was the white community "entitled to take such measures," the editors asked, if their numbers did not "predominate"? "The sobering answer is *Yes*—the White community is so entitled because, for the time being, it is the advanced race."[76] An editor like Bozell might worry that this sounded seditious, that it was doubtful that "we," as conservative intellectuals, "can successfully do battle against the Establishment while our allegiance to the Constitution is an 'open question.'" But that did not stop the conservative intellectual energy mounting behind the defense of "massive resistance" or from calls to break laws.[77]

The southern cry in the backwoods was rising up, and conservatives believed it was time to explain why it had to be the case. They hoped to back up the cause of "massive resistance" and justify anger and a white populist revolt against the judiciary (as well as against ordinary black citizens). They had found *their* movement. Some conservative writers, such as J. J. Kilpatrick, saw the threat of disorder and chaos heating up as the civil rights movement became more active and believed this served as sufficient reason to push back against King's argument for full equality. "Manifestly, race-mixing of certain schools now leads to knifings, dynamitings, and other forms of violence." He went on to explain that "if the courts insist upon unyielding enforcement of the newly created rights of Negro pupils, the communities of the South may be reduced to chaos and blood may flow ankle-deep in the gutters." That sort of violence would be justified, Kilpatrick hinted, if the courts and black citizens insisted on changing the terms of southern society.[78]

Other writers turned openly seditious in the face of Little Rock. Some believed Eisenhower's stationing of troops in Arkansas was intended to prompt mobs and thus justify further strong-arm tactics. For the conservative mind, the Civil War had been reinvented in the streets of the South. Ike, in the minds of *National Review* editors, was "the prisoner of the nation's most dangerous and extreme Liberal ideologues" who wanted to trample the "division of power" between the states and the federal government and between executive and judiciary power. Ike was unleashing something that would lead "ineluctably to the release of the civil war potential."[79] Indeed, the "bayonets" of liberalism—the doctrine's need for force—had been exposed by Little Rock. There was now "in Little Rock" an "army of occupation."[80] Frank Meyer started hinting that nullification might be the right weapon for the South to start using.[81] Southerners, another writer pointed out, were tired of "being attacked, pushed around, scorned, ridiculed" by the North and especially liberal intellectuals. What the South offered was a society based on "inequalities" that could challenge the liberal ideal of equality. The southerners became "the least 'other-directed' citizens in this Republic," meaning the most radical nonconformists who held out a political alternative and perhaps a revolution against liberalism. They were the true representatives of Buckley's rebels. What could be more rebellious than the Stars and Bars?[82]

Sedition. Rebellion. War. These were now features of the conservative mind confronting Little Rock. The attitude could be gleaned from a writer who described "Washington as an alien power, as alien in a way as Moscow" and "submission to an alien power" as "unworthy and evil."[83] It is no surprise that the conservative mind—rebellious and pugnacious in its style—would find itself in league with the southern rebel type. Stars and Bars and tough-ass rebellion constituted a firm foundation for conservative rebellion, much more potent than the visages of Brando or Dean, more radical than the Beats who were dropping out and doing drugs, more tough than Norman Mailer's hipsters who were bashing in the heads of candy store owners. "Massive resistance" was also a political tradition that emphasized a radical form of decentralization that sprang from the southern argument for states' rights. And though the civil rights movement (and then the New Left) could claim participatory democracy as its own ideal, it was matched by the participatory democracy of Little Rock's white citizens. The southern manifesto that declared war against the civil rights movement and that was signed by numerous elected officials served as a crucial document in the history of the conservative mind—one that had a great deal of political energy already behind it.[84]

The Southern Agrarians had cherished a South of gentlemen and small farmers toiling away and nurturing a way of life of tradition and religion. But the South championed by postwar intellectuals was, by historical necessity, a place of stone-throwing mobs, "massive resistance," and battles over racial justice. It was symbolized by the Dixiecrats who bolted the Democratic Party in favor of a conservative position on business and a reactionary one on civil rights in 1948, by the formation of White Citizens' Councils against the civil rights movement throughout the 1950s and 1960s, and by George Wallace's stance in the door of the University of Alabama in 1963 to defend segregation. Down the road these acts would culminate in Wallace's political move-ment, during the late 1960s, that chided "liberal leftwing punks" and a "judicial dictatorship" and that appealed in the North and South alike. It perfected itself in Richard Nixon's "southern strategy" for the Republican Party, begun in 1968 and carried to fruition today in the "red state" consolidation of the South. Stated forthrightly, this was an intellectual move from Southern Agrarianism to southern strategy, to the growing realization that conservatives could crack the Democratic South and start to gain votes there if they took advantage of the liberal pledge to create civil rights for African Americans. The conservative mind did not find it difficult to stand for universal values while situat-ing them in actual historical and empirical practices. But it was a shift from ideas to political strategy—a shift that would grow more pronounced during the 1960s with the presidential success of Richard Nixon.[85]

LOOKING ELSEWHERE AND MORE FRUITFULLY: FROM "REMNANT" TO REBELS WITH A FORWARD MARCH

The conservative embrace of the American South and "massive resistance" would of course end in defeat. After all, the govern-ment implemented the *Brown v. Board of Education* decision (albeit slowly), and this civil rights victory was followed by sweeping legislative success in favor of voting rights and desegregation in 1964–1965. But the spirit behind "massive resistance" would live on in the conservative mind and in the successes of southern politicians turning Republican. It made clear that rebellion, including citizens massing in the streets and threatening to battle their own government, had become a constitutive element in the conservative mind. Nevertheless, supporting white southern resistance to black equality was too reactionary in style—too defensive of the status quo and not forward-looking enough—to provide conservatives with the necessary energy to move ahead in their struggles. Reaction did not fit the mood of the late 1950s as the United States transitioned into a new decade. Hopefulness crept into American culture—a thawing of the Cold War and a search for new leadership coming from a new generation, eventually captured, most evocatively, in President John F. Kennedy's election. The conservative mind was not hopeful about Kennedy, of course, but it was hopeful and forward-looking about conservative ideals having their own future triumph some time.

Strange as it might sound, conservative intellectuals helped nurture the "new radicalism" that would define American life during the 1960s. Numerous histories of the period make clear that the decade's tumult and rebellious atmosphere actually started during the 1950s: the Beat writers of the 1950s foresaw the counterculture of the 1960s, and social critics of the 1950s (David Riesman and C. Wright Mills) laid the basis for student discontent during the 1960s. When Buckley penned *God and Man at Yale*, he too was unleashing hope for a new radicalism among younger followers. And he heard echoes when he shouted. For instance, the editors of *National Review* would praise the Midwest Federation of College Young Republican Clubs meeting in 1957, because the students assembled there openly opposed Eisenhower.[86] Perhaps youth would save the Republicans from themselves. Certainly, when Young Americans for Freedom (YAF) formed in 1960 under Buckley's leadership, the mood grew ecstatic. Finally there was a youth conservative

group whose ideas reflected Buckley's own and whose membership would grow in coming years. Perhaps the "personal power-
lessness" that students complained about and that Buckley
dissected was now a thing of the past.[87]

Conservative social criticism would help nurture this shift,
as liberal social criticism would lay the ground for the New Left.
Conservative love for free markets led quite naturally to a critique of bureaucracy that spoke to numerous anxieties spreading
throughout American culture during the 1950s. It also played
well when Americans became used to reading popular jeremiads
about the conformity of the white-collar classes who were
working for large bureaucratic corporations and living in face-
less suburbs. The "affluent society," as the liberal economist John
Kenneth Galbraith called it, defined much social criticism during the time. "Impersonality" and "alienation" became popular
terms. Americans heard about "other-directed" individualism,
the "organization man," and conformity. The term "mass society" found common expression in popular conversations about
what was wrong with America, suggesting a fear of homogene-
ity represented by the proliferation of television, Muzak, comic
books, and movies. As a historian of the 1950s and liberal
thought points out: "Liberated from the assumptions of the
1930s, many intellectuals in the 1950s attacked the social order
not because it was politically unjust or economically oppressive,
but because it seemed impersonal, bureaucratic, and inhumane."
Boredom and frustration with "growing up absurd" in a culture
of the "gray flannel suit" helped fuel the writing of many best-
selling paperback books. This discontent provided much of the
energy of the student revolt to come.[88]

Conservatives contributed to this growing feeling. The conservative critique of modernity—of its flabbiness and obsession
with comfort and prosperity—helped buttress a wider critique
of 1950s consumer culture. Russell Kirk could sound an awful
lot like Galbraith when he bemoaned "immediate gratification"

and "the new Pontiac beside the decrepit shack." Kirk scoffed at "shoddy new bungalows, juke joints, concrete, billboards." America was witnessing, in his mind, an "Age of Gluttony," a time when "buying and consuming" had become king. And affluence and consumerism appeared little more than con jobs—doping citizens into submission and false and distracting desires.[89]

Conservatives were quick to point out that conformity was a by-product of liberalism—not capitalism. Liberals, flabby as they were, provided no deeper meaning to life; they offered only a culture of complacency and "comfort." Richard Weaver offered "the strenuous ideals of life" as an alternative to liberalism that could foster resistance against the "natural, indolent, ease-loving, and complacent self" that liberalism promised and that a consumer culture had democratized for the masses. Rebellion against the "other-directed society" meant a radical individualism (tempered by religious faith) that could buck the system. True rebellion would take on a conservative cast in America's new mass society.[90] Buckley put it this way: "There is no Liberal vision. And so long as there is not, there is no call for that kind of passionate commitment that stirs the political blood." Mass conformity promised nothing, liberalism promised less. The only ones willing to offer a passionate exit from the conformist 1950s were conservatives.[91]

Some conservative critics expanded their critique of President Eisenhower into a broader critique of American culture during the 1950s. In doing this, they were part of the mainstream of intellectual life that saw linkages between social conformity and middle-of-the-road politics. Ike's softness became especially tiresome during the end of the decade, as lame-duck presidencies are prone to be. Eisenhower's era offered a "peculiar horror," in the words of Frank Meyer. Meyer worried that "nothing can break into the drugged dream of Moderation and Prosperity." The real rebel of the 1950s for Meyer was McCarthy, who offered a "substantial challenge to the reign of complacent self-approving compromise with evil" that had taken hold in America.[92] Now, Meyer hoped, the winds of change were starting to blow. It would be easy to see the events that helped to keep a conservative social critic looking for alternatives to liberalism: Senator Joe McCarthy's one-man war against communism and liberals, southern rebels' "massive resistance" against the civil rights movement, and then the formation of right-wing student organizations like YAF. The conformist culture of America, though it had beaten McCarthy and southern resistance against the civil rights movement, seemed to be getting a fair challenge.

Others continued Buckley's critique of academe and worked from there to a wider critique of conformist America. Universities for Russell Kirk were vast, growing bureaucracies that were increasingly inhumane and depersonalized. He noticed that student apathy at big state universities got worse as time proceeded. The "progressive" education that taught young people life-adjustment and career skills numbed their minds. And so there might be seeds for a youth revolt, and perhaps conservatives could push it in a conservative direction (as Paul Goodman was hoping that he could push it in his own left-anarchist direction). After all, students faced a university culture growing fat not from private donations but from federal dollars funding Cold War research, making it easier to see how Buckley's personal war against Yale could be turned to distinct conservative advantage. Students might aim their anger against what Kirk called the "Federal Educational Boondoggle."[93]

With all of this in mind, it is no surprise that conservatives added to the general feeling that there was a "new radicalism" afoot in the early 1960s. Conservatives were not the Beats or the Hipsters.[94] But having grown gloomy about Republican Party prospects, they looked outside of traditional political forms and hoped for cultural change. They looked for alternatives to "a homogeneous mass of identical individuals" and the "sterile modern mass mind." Against what David Riesman labeled "other-directed" individuals—those who took their cues less from themselves than from others they worked with in large bureaucracies—conservatives articulated a rebellion of "inner-directed" radical individualists. The new radicals of the Left would also complain about a "liberal establishment," but when conservatives complained, it resonated deeper. They were more hopeful about a revolution of the young against a decrepit liberal elite and in favor of what would be called a "new sensibility."[95]

When Buckley published *Up from Liberalism* in 1959, Irving Kristol (then a liberal with conservative leanings and someone discussed in the next chapter) pointed out that "far from being recognizably conservative," Buckley was a "gay dissenter" who shared "more in common with C. Wright Mills than any other contemporary writer one can think of."[96] Mills, of course, was the key theorist of the New Left (writing about the "New Left" at the time that Buckley published his book) and was the leading critic of the "end of ideology" thesis. He saw Bell's idea as an ideology itself—as a technocratic, lifeless justification of the managerial welfare state. Mills wanted young people to bust out of the conformity of Eisenhower's America and the white-collar prison. So too Buckley. The "end of ideology" was a myth for both men. But Buckley had a better ear for the future's rumblings, and he was well poised for the era of the 1960s.

Two

The Big Chill That Set Fires

Having been for two decades a mordant critic
of what is foolishly called the higher learning
in America, I confess to relishing somewhat . . . the fulfillment of my predictions
and the present plight of the educationist
Establishment. I even own to a sneaking
sympathy, after a fashion, with the campus
revolutionaries.   —Russell Kirk, 1969

THINK ABOUT THE 1960s, and certain people
and larger-than-life figures probably come to mind: John F.
Kennedy, Lyndon Baines Johnson, Malcolm X, Abbie Hoffman,
Jerry Rubin, Allen Ginsberg. All men associated with the Left
or liberalism. Perhaps some intellectuals also come to mind,
especially those who sympathized with the growing student
protest movements of the decade: Norman Mailer, Theodore
Roszak, Paul Goodman, Herbert Marcuse. Images might bounce
around too: love beads, tie-dyed clothing, Woodstock, university
protests, inner city riots. And, of course, the soundtrack for all
this would be provided by acid rocksters like Jefferson Airplane
or Jimi Hendrix. Increasingly, though, historians have provided a
fuller picture of the decade by bringing in figures associated not
with liberalism, leftism, or the counterculture but with the
American Right: William F. Buckley and Barry Goldwater first
and foremost, as well as neoconservative intellectuals like Irving
Kristol and Norman Podhoretz. Though this side of the sixties

lacks a soundtrack, it is replete with images of Republican kids decked out in ties rallying for Young Americans for Freedom (YAF) or attending Barry Goldwater events somewhere in Orange County, California.

We are gradually overcoming our long-lived misperception that the 1960s was a springtime of the Left and liberalism. And that is true even if we continue to believe, as we should, that a new "mood" dominated the 1960s and gave it a distinct feel—the feel of youthful rebellion smacking up against the boring, corporate, bureaucratic existence (perceived or otherwise) of the 1950s. In understanding this dynamism and change—what authors like Morris Dickstein and Ronald Berman have called a "new sensibility"—it behooves us to continue to focus on the Right. This "new sensibility" of the 1960s informed both sides of the political spectrum, cutting across ideological differences. The term "new sensibility" might sound vague, but its outlines can be quickly drawn. It has less to do with political than cultural radicalism, sparked by anger at middle-class conformity and a search for new forms of expression, and more to do with an embrace of "utopian" ideals lying outside the humdrum elements of electoral politics. This new sensibility exploded bureaucratic and electoral politics for radical populism and a celebration of democratic participation as an end in itself—as a key way to find "authentic" experience. It raised questions about unified or objective interpretations of reality and pioneered an intellectual style we now label postmodernism—a worldview that embraces multiple viewpoints versus overarching claims to absolute truth. Expressiveness—witnessed not just in rock music and drugs but also in the "new journalism" movement that made the feeling of the writer matter as much as the reporting of facts—became the sensibility's most cherished value.[1]

The new sensibility emerged within a distinct historical context and nurtured a specific take on the recent past, especially a narrative that depicted the 1950s as a decade of dullness, conformity, stagnation, and all things phony and the 1960s as a time of openness and freedom. It drew energy from the baby boom generation that wanted something more than the careerism and comfort of the postwar years—a comfort that might have appealed to its parents who experienced economic depression and sacrifice necessary to wage a long, grueling war, but failed a hungrier generation who rejected comfort for excitement and experimentation. The baby boomers—a generation that talked about itself incessantly—fueled the decade's "new sensibility" in rebellion against an older generation and a conception of the 1950s as a time of conformity and dullness.

A good starting point to understand how conservative intellectuals contributed to this new sensibility is *Revolt on the Campus,* a book published in 1961 by M. Stanton Evans, a young midwestern journalist whose feet were planted strongly in right-wing politics and who cut his teeth first reading and then writing for the *National Review.* "It is the conservative who is young, angry, déclassé" on the American college campus, Evans explained. Angry rebellion on the Right might have sounded counterintuitive to readers, but it shouldn't, he argued. For instance, the rebels now taken as forerunners of the 1960s counterculture, Beat writers like Jack Kerouac and Allen Ginsberg who denounced the conformity of 1950s America, were, for Evans, protoconservatives—especially Kerouac, whose "chief hate was Washington bureaucracy; second to that, Liberals; then cops," making his politics (if such a thing existed) more libertarian than leftist (on this point, Evans was prescient, as Kerouac became blatantly conservative during the 1960s, blathering conservative ideas, ironically enough, on William F. Buckley's *Firing Line* show). Young people were attending college in larger numbers, and they faced—as William F. Buckley had already made clear— a liberal professoriate trying to cram its values down their throats. Evans wrote: "Liberalism is the orthodoxy on American campuses . . ., it has sought to repress conservative dissent." To be conservative and young constituted an inevitable act of angry rebellion. A young conservative on almost any college campus faced "a machine for molding students into acceptance of Liberal values." Evans bemoaned the "still-born generation" of the 1950s as too complacent, a complaint that the writers of the Port Huron Statement—the founding document of the New Left, or at least its most prominent organization, Students for a Democratic Society (SDS)—would echo when they worried in 1962 about a new generation "bred in at least modest comfort" who "began maturing in complacency."[2]

Evans started with the "machine" of bureaucratic academe but did not finish there. With the yarn of academe, he wove a wider web that included Hollywood, the mass media, and the book publishing industry. All of these institutions constituted a "liberal establishment"—a term Evans used in 1965 in ways similar to the New Left's complaints about the "system" or "corporate liberalism." Adopting sociological categories developed by David Riesman, Evans explained that angry, young conservatives were "inner-directed" rebels fed up with "other-directed" conformists who were afraid to challenge liberal shibboleths on college campuses or the political center in American politics that had grown comfortable with New Deal inheritances. The liberal bureaucrat, the staid university administrator, the left-wing journalist, the egghead intellectual—all of these figures constituted something bigger, a massive conspiracy against conservative authenticity and anger. This sentiment animated not just Evans's writing but also the continuing activities of the Intercollegiate Society of Individualists (founded in 1953) and the Young Americans for Freedom (YAF), an organization that had formed just before *Revolt on the Campus* hit bookstores. At the time Evans's book emerged, one journalist felt comfortable describing "America's Angry Young Men" waging war against a "liberal establishment." And these young men were of the Right, not the Left.[3]

Conservative intellectuals would not welcome all of the decade's developments. They had already recoiled at the civil rights movement that emerged during the 1950s, and they would later shudder at protests against the House Un-American Activities Committee (HUAC), inner city riots, and most features of the anti–Vietnam War protests. Much of the decade's rebellion went in a direction different from the kind Evans called for in 1961. It would attack the liberal professoriate and media but predominantly from the Left. Nonetheless, conservative thinkers contributed to and shared much more with the atmosphere of the decade's new sensibility than we typically think. And the cultural residues from the decade helped define the conservative intellectual movement in ways we have yet to understand.

Youth (and Goldwater) Will Make the Revolution

Evans was onto something very real—not just a sensibility but the growing energy in Young Americans for Freedom that had formed at the decade's beginning in 1960. When conservative students gathered at William Buckley's estate to draft the Sharon Statement in September 1960, they helped nurture a conservative movement beyond the pages of the *National Review*. The Sharon Statement was nowhere near as sophisticated as SDS's Port Huron Statement (which was released two years later). It was too short, with declarative sentence piled on top of declarative sentence (all sounding as if they should be followed with an exclamation point), and overly simplistic about its libertarianism (a philosophy that comes easily to the young). But that did not matter in the long run. YAF drew on the energy of young people who had grown disaffected with the centrism of the Republican Party, and it became the leading conservative youth organization that grew in size and influence throughout the 1960s. Some of the students who attended the gathering at

Buckley's home had been active earlier in defending Cold War loyalty oaths on college campuses (instituted as part of the National Defense Act) and arguing against liberal professors who worried that such oaths violated civil liberties and academic freedom. Some had defended HUAC against early New Left protests. Others had taken up M. Stanton Evans's call to fight the influence of liberal professors on campus (foreseeing the activism of David Horowitz thirty years later). Even with splits and factions as well as oddball leaders, YAF grew in membership throughout the 1960s by recruiting predominantly lower-class and Catholic students into its ranks. It certainly outpaced the growth of SDS, its New Left counterpart.[4]

Buckley was clearly excited about the Sharon conference. And it was not just that there were generational successors for his own arguments and ideas. It was that the attitude of the young people gathered at Sharon represented a change in the postwar conservative mind. Buckley explained: "What is so striking in the students who met at Sharon is their appetite for power. Ten years ago, the struggle seemed so long, so endless, that we did not dream of victory. The difference in psychological attitude is tremendous." The term "psychological attitude" is important: a hard-to-define change in mood was occurring in 1960, one that was connected to a sense of growing influence. A long-term struggle seemed to be emerging, with fresh faces ensuring it rejuvenation as it moved forward. The impression was no longer just of thinking—the dominant mood of the 1950s—but the sense of *action*. Although Goldwater would help push the Republicans to the right, YAF'ers could nurture right-wing student activism that built networks from below. Students could protest things like Kennedy's Test Ban Treaty and other attempts to thaw out the Cold War. Politics might not be drifting their way at the presidential level yet, but YAF'ers ensured that the intellectuals at the *National Review* were not the only representatives of conservatism during the decade.[5]

Four years after the Sharon Statement, most of Buckley's young protégés in YAF entered the campaign offices of Barry Goldwater. Goldwater's 1964 run for the presidency was the most important event of the conservative movement during the decade, and it had a distinct and profound effect on the postwar conservative mind. Goldwater successfully won the presidential candidacy against the "liberal establishment" within the Republican Party, personified in Goldwater's primary campaign opponent, Nelson Rockefeller (a divorced man with gobs of money). Goldwater mobilized existing grassroots networks and built some of his own in order to wage his campaign. And he gained assistance from political figures who would eventually help contribute to and benefit from the long-term drift to the right in America. After all, Ronald Reagan gave one of the most inspirational speeches for the Goldwater campaign—quoted more often than Goldwater's own speeches—and then won the California governorship in 1966 and the presidency in 1980, with much the same message as Goldwater, but with a dash of smiling optimism added.[6]

Goldwater's candidacy created a tension in the conservative mind that would last a long time after he lost the election. It grew from a simple fact: power beckoned. Conservative thinkers started to wonder if they might win political influence rather than remain outside electoral politics and pursue the freewheeling thinking that marked the 1950s. In 1958, when Republicans had already moved to the center and wound up losing Congress in midterm elections, conservative intellectuals grew morose. "American conservatism has no political organization and no political leadership," Brent Bozell declared sadly. But then conservative intellectuals watched excitedly as Barry Goldwater—a man not from the Northeast but from the Southwest of the United States—rose to prominence, leading opposition to the civil rights movement and then publishing a manifesto in 1960 with ideas they helped develop. Suddenly, attitudes about politics shifted. By 1963, as Goldwater won support within the

Republican Party, conservative thinkers at the *National Review* grew exuberant about the possibility of winning "the solid South" to their own party and their own definition of conservatism. Instead of sitting on the sidelines and developing philosophical principles, conservative intellectuals turned strategic. Their earlier confidence that they could transform the country appeared in Goldwater's suntanned face beaming out at cheering crowds. They certainly were not "remnants" clutching on to defeated ideas.[7]

Goldwater was a new politician who led with old ideas. He had published *The Conscience of a Conservative* in 1960, a manifesto that sold well and enthused supporters in the conservative movement (largely ghost-written by Brent Bozell).[8] The book was rather slim, a mere 120 pages of big print that added little to conservative ideas not already gleaned from a quick read of the *National Review*. Goldwater outlined the principle of individual freedom and then argued that the federal government should not intervene in society—even for the sake of racial integration (which on its own terms he did not oppose). He then attacked labor unions and ended with a call for a strong anticommunist foreign policy. Reading Goldwater was like reading a thinner version of Frank Meyer mixed with James Burnham.[9] So it is not surprising to find Meyer, for one, ready to hitch his hopes to Goldwater's campaign. He believed when Goldwater won the presidency—something he thought would happen right up until the first numbers showed crushing defeat—"the energies of the long-thwarted people" would create a populist upsurge. For Meyer, the term "conservative" had grown in respectability earlier, but something nevertheless changed when Barry Goldwater started to use the term. It went "from being a curse word, a designation from which all but the most intrepid fled" to being "a roaring challenge to the established power and the established aridities of the post-Roosevelt era." Goldwater had made conservatism *real*.[10]

Goldwater had also made conservatism more palatable by adopting the decade's new sensibility—especially a style of authenticity. He spoke off the cuff, offering strange ruminations in public that puzzled listeners (blabbing about weaknesses in the American missile system or about how America had experimented with "socialism and communism and egalitarianism and monarchy and everything else, arriving" finally "at our constitutional republic" two hundred years ago). He was a cowboy from the West who spoke honestly. Straight talk—including strange statements—proved Goldwater was his own man, not a typical pol groomed for the television cameras.[11] He was gruff, honest, and authentic. Goldwater lashed out at the phony and flabby feel of America's consumer culture. He told a television audience: "If we in this hour of world crisis are content to amuse ourselves with the material luxuries freedom has produced, we stand guilty of trading the future of all mankind for a brief moment of uncertain safety for our generation." His campaign became an idealist crusade against the staid conformity of American consumerism and an ossified "Republican Establishment," replicating the 1960s spirit of authenticity and utopia against bureaucratic and traditional political forms—or what Goldwater himself called the threat of America's becoming a "regimented society."[12]

When Goldwater went to the Republican Party convention in 1964, he was set to make a big speech, and it became a speech that is now famous. At the time, it personified not only his authenticity but his spirit of brash rebellion and the propensity the conservative mind had developed throughout the 1950s and that it would hold on to from that moment onward—a love of speaking in bombastic and apocalyptic tones. The convention moment became iconic, as Barry Goldwater looked at his roaring fans and bellowed: "I would remind you that extremism in the defense of liberty is no vice! And let me remind you also— that moderation in the pursuit of justice is no virtue." These became famous words, whose message is easily forgotten. They said to the outside world: *Yes, we are bold, and, no, we won't settle for anything less than total transformation of our society.* This was the apocalyptic sentiment James Burnham and Whittaker Chambers had handed down to the conservative movement, absolutist principles justifying an open-ended determination of means (including warfare). Conservatives adopted a mindset of permanent war that defined a great deal of American political culture during the decade. Much the same sentiment was eventually heard in the angry speeches made by the Black Panthers and the Weather Underground. Goldwater's speech was a utopian call to arms, a message to the true believers that the candidate was an authentic rebel willing to give it to the man by bucking the complacency of the age and his own party. This attitude might have helped lose him the election (LBJ's staff believed that), but it sent a clear cultural message about conservatism and held out promise for long-term transformation. It also made clear that conservatives had imbibed and contributed to the utopian spirit normally associated with the 1960s.[13]

Goldwater's boldness and authenticity required the *National Review* to spend a lot of time writing defenses for his more extremist statements—including his call to sell off the TVA and abolish Social Security (the latter being of the most popular legacies of the New Deal). So much energy went into defending Goldwater and explaining his quixotic views, that the *National Review*'s editors had to clarify that their magazine was not a "campaign organ."[14] They still thought in larger terms than just winning elections. Goldwater's campaign, in fact, made explicit the long-term aims of the postwar conservative mind. The most important issue of all was the question of whether or not the liberal media would treat Goldwater fairly. "How can Goldwater speak his mind," the editors wondered, when liberals would pounce on any misstatement he might make?[15] M. Stanton Evans believed that unless conservatives reformed the liberal media—a

goal that seemed to assume a long-term strategy—a candidate
like Goldwater could never succeed. Conservative intellectuals
could shill for Goldwater in the short term while connecting his
candidacy to the wider goal of transforming American political
culture. Criticisms of the liberal media would stick in the cranial
fixtures of the postwar conservative mind and would continue to
grow from this point onward.[16]

Endorsing Goldwater ended the aloofness toward electoral
politics that marked the 1950s, but it was also a sign of the growing confidence of the postwar conservative mind. Goldwater's
campaign did not change conservative ideas as much as made
clear a grassroots movement ready to act on ideas. Conservatives
like Buckley could now safely consider themselves "movement
intellectuals," as some on the Left would call themselves at the
same time considering the rise of student activism and groups
like SDS. Although the *National Review* began as a podium to
appeal to and win over intellectuals, it now projected a more
populist posture, previewed already by its praise for Senator
McCarthy, support for "massive resistance" in the South, and
the energy exhibited in young Republicans pushing their party
further to the right. Goldwater was the Right's populist inaugu-
ral moment. Many right-wing intellectuals started to see their
dreams coming to fruition and gathering energy from below, not
just from the pages of the *National Review.*

As much as strategy became more important in 1964, debating ideas continued to be crucial as well. In fact, the 1960s reen-
ergized the conservative intellectual movement. Ironically, the
rise of the student New Left and high-profile protests at the
University of California, Berkeley in 1964 (the Free Speech
Movement) and Columbia University in 1968 helped charge up
conservative thinkers. The centrality of student protests in
defining the politics and chaos of the decade made young conservative thinkers all that more important, for they would provide
a counternarrative about the decade's disturbances. A newer

generation of conservative intellectuals sometimes wrote for the *National Review,* but they also received support from other institutions like the Philadelphia Society and the Intercollegiate Society of Individualists (ISI). In 1965, ISI decided to publish a new journal for young academics and intellectuals, the *Intercollegiate Review,* targeted especially at the growing numbers of college students in the United States. The publication was not widely circulated, but it was certainly a sign of growth in the ranks. Russell Kirk, who wrote for it while maintaining his column at *National Review,* believed that the birth of new "campus conservative journals" showed that the real energy in political thought remained on the right, even as politics drifted to the left in the mid-1960s.[17]

Younger conservative intellectuals helped criticize but also explain why American college campuses—prosperous and growing in importance throughout the decade—became hotbeds for radical protest. It was easy. After all, Buckley had slammed the university as a source of liberal indoctrination, and Russell Kirk had condemned the federal "boondoggle"—especially contracts for defense-related research—that helped beef up the "multiversity" of the 1960s. Now the results of bureaucratic growth were plain to see. Student protesters expressed alienation about life within the university—large classes increasingly taught by underpaid graduate students, students rarely knowing their teachers' names, increasing numbers of administrators populating universities. When Mario Savio, leader of the Free Speech Movement at Berkeley, condemned the "impersonal bureaucracy" and America's "utopia of sterilized, automated contentment," conservative writers listened intently.[18] A writer in *Intercollegiate Review* explained that students rightfully felt "cheated" by college experience.[19] The New Left raised serious questions about the purposes of education, and conservatives provided answers. Some believed writers like Paul Goodman had increased in popularity for legitimate reasons, because they addressed students who were "fed up with the bureaucracy of the multiversity."[20] Conservatives could cheer this on and support student protesters demanding political decentralization as a solution to impersonal bureaucracy. *Intercollegiate Review* writers pointed out that New Left critics came to similar conclusions as Barry Goldwater. One went so far as to claim "obvious areas of agreement" between the New Left and the Old Right.[21]

Students were not just raising questions about impersonal bureaucracies; they were raising questions about the politics of knowledge and modern science's claim to objectivity. New Left students protested the university's role in defense-related research, especially in the hard sciences. The ivory tower no longer seemed "objective" but rather complicit with a military machine that had embarked on an increasingly unpopular war. Noam Chomsky, a young left-wing scholar with growing sympathies for student protesters, condemned the "technical intelligentsia" and its pretension of "scholarly detachment." The neutrality of science played into the hands of those prosecuting the war, and Chomsky scrutinized the pretense of objectivity made by the "new mandarins."[22] Chomsky's protests were similar to those of conservative intellectuals. Writers in the *Intercollegiate Review* believed the Western project of science—with its amoral stance of objectivity—was collapsing around them. One condemned, à la Chomsky, "irresponsible" social scientists who seemed to "play a large, in many respects decisive, and possibly disastrous part in our military planning" in Vietnam.[23] Another condemned intellectuals who had turned "away from moral judgment to the insistence on science and methodology."[24] Science and bureaucratic planning—housed most auspiciously in the multiversities of the age—were amoral and dangerous. Indeed, M. Stanton Evans pointed out: "The planners have tried to homogenize us into a kind of obedient tapioca, pliable to the touch of experts. These manipulations have angered the libertarian nerve of American students and supplied the new left with its most effective entry to the campus."[25] Rebellion might have moved to the left since he wrote *Revolt on the Campus* in 1961, Evans admitted, but the source of its anger could easily be viewed as property of the Right.

Of course, student protesters took things too far for the young conservative intelligentsia. At Berkeley, for instance, they engaged in "body rhetoric"—a dangerous form of physical resistance that easily degenerated into violence.[26] But the real problem with student protesters was that they misunderstood the roots of the "malaise" that the modern university generated. At the center was the problem that Buckley diagnosed fifteen years earlier—the problem of what one graduate student, writing in the pages of *Intercollegiate Review*, called "academic freedom," a "slogan which thinly, if at all, veils the thoroughgoing relativism of the 'learned' community."[27] In explaining the shortcomings of the New Left, M. Stanton Evans pushed this argument one step further. He suggested that the New Left *sounded* "very anti-liberal and pro-freedom." From the conservative perspective, their revolt played itself out in a totalitarian direction. The New Left, for Evans, constituted the foot soldiers who extended the fascistic essence of liberalism. Liberals had strengthened the state and had thus "paved the way for an American Nazism," and so the New Left became the equivalent of Nazi youth. Evans compared the SDS takeover of Columbia to the "basic method of the Nazi faction" to "hurl itself against the existing political machinery until it broke."[28] After all, student protests and pressures simply exposed the absurd freedoms allowed for by the modern university. Evans spelled out the wild antinomies entering conservative thought at this time: a love for the New Left's energetic rebellion and the enemies it shared with the Right, mixed with a recoiling at the substantive politics student protesters promoted.

Even with Evans's arguments in mind, the energy of the student protests continued to provide inspiration for the Old Right.

One conservative sociology professor would explain youthful protests this way: "In America, youth was dehumanized by the mass manipulation of appetites and pre-aged by conformity with the values of the middle-aged." Still another writer from the Right suggested that the New Left's fear of the United States's "rapidly becoming a bureaucratic corporate state" was legitimate. The term "bureaucratic corporate state" sounded an awful lot like what writers at *Studies on the Left* described, around the same time, as "corporate liberalism." The only difference was that the same young, right-wing intellectual—sounding a lot like Evans—complained that discontent was only associated with the Left. "Why don't" angry New Left students "credit Barry Goldwater specifically and conservatives generally for first discovering the problems they now shout about?" he asked. After all, the Right had ignited the new sensibility of the time, no matter how much student protesters ignored this.[29]

Both Right and Left stoked and fed off the growing alienation among students. In the winter of 1969, a year after Columbia University was overrun by leading SDS activists and student protests turned more violent, Russell Kirk could write: "I even own to a sneaking sympathy, after a fashion, with the campus revolutionaries." He could "sympathize with the mood of rebellion. For two decades, I have been declaring that most colleges and universities are sunk in decadence. Against that decadence, the confused outcries of the New Left people are a reaction." Not that he agreed with their solution, but their sentiment made sense. Another conservative thinker even saw something good in the work of Herbert Marcuse—a radical, German-born philosopher who permanently relocated in the United States and criticized a technocratic and "one-dimensional society" of consumerism and corporate bureaucracy. Marcuse was talking up a "great refusal" on the part of young students against cultural homogenization and sterility. Though the *Intercollegiate Review* writer condemned almost the entirety of

Marcuse's theory, he admitted that this paragon of New Left ideas had exposed the "hypocrisies" of America and the fact that "freedom merely allows us to pursue ends that are worthless," meaning the fruitless pursuit of more material goods. This merger of far-Left and far-Right on the plane of ideas even found expression in the world of activism. Some YAF'ers staged sit-ins—a symbol of the civil rights movement and antiwar protests—at SDS offices to protest the organization's policies. And when the Vietnam protests focused on antidraft activism, a faction of YAF'ers pledged their libertarian support. Authenticity and personal freedom from the state demanded such consistency on the part of some young men of ideas and activists. Perhaps the funniest example of all this was Antoni Gollan's exploration of "conservative potheads" in a 1968 issue of the *National Review.* The Right found some commonality with the counterculture, a movement most would suspect it detested.[30]

Too much can be made of this, of course. There were plenty of YAF'ers who were following Barry Goldwater's counsel and adopting "Why Not Victory" for their slogan about Vietnam (a difficult slogan to shout when body counts were mounting), and James Burnham would call for invading China and using chemical weapons on Vietnam, rather than scaling back the war. The pages of the *National Review,* during the late 1960s, published numerous comics that made fun of the style of New Left protests. (A typical one shows two kids with protest signs looking at a headline that states "LBJ Stops Bombing." One protester turns to the other and says: "After all these years it's going to be difficult to find something to do on Sundays.")[31]

The Old Right would continue with its populist talk—echoed in Richard Nixon's praise for the "silent majority"—while waiting out the storm of the late 1960s. Better to allow the lunacies of the New Left—the student takeovers of universities, the gun-toting antics of the Black Panther Party, the inner city riots, and the violence of the Weather Underground—to piss off middle America and help delegitimize liberal leaders like LBJ. Recoiling in horror as society seemed to come apart served the Right well ("the whole world is watching" strategy of the New Left helping the Right more in the long run than it did the protesters who chanted those words). Right-wing students and intellectuals could hunker down and condemn left-wing anti-Vietnam protests and the snobbery of the student movement that purportedly looked down on the "hardhats" being sent to war (most of YAF's members themselves came from working-class backgrounds). Articles on the urban riots and talk of "law and order" dominated the pages of the *National Review* from 1968 to 1969. They were joined by a new set of intellectuals during this time as well: A group of "neoconservatives" who reacted against the Old Right and warned against populism. Before the postwar conservative mind could consolidate around the New Right and populism, it had to get through this intellectual interruption.[32]

THE NEOCONSERVATIVE INTERVENTION AND DETOUR

The term "neoconservative" refers to a group of predominantly New York and Jewish thinkers who had shifted from the Trotskyist Left in the 1930s to the liberal center during the 1950s and then to Nixonian and moderate conservatism during the 1970s. These writers famously complained about being "mugged" by the 1960s—shocked by university takeovers (the sort that still warmed the heart of Russell Kirk), inner city riots, and the rise of black power. They worried about a bloated American welfare state that could not accommodate "rising entitlements." Neoconservatives looked at the world and defended the principle of anticommunism, even as it became associated with America's quagmire in Vietnam. Numerous historians recount how these thinkers helped energize the conservative intellectual movement by providing new methodologies—especially social science research that was less moralistic than Old Right arguments. Being Jewish, they also helped diversify what was had been largely a Catholic and Protestant movement.[33]

In the context of any story about the conservative intellectual movement, neoconservative figures like Irving Kristol and Norman Podhoretz loom large. They deserve the status, but not as much as is sometimes given. The neoconservative imagination had limitations, its strengths and weaknesses being married. Neoconservatives were out of the fold—too cosmopolitan, erudite, and complex to be effective spokespeople for an *American* version of conservatism. They had an aura of New York City about them—a quality that would not appeal to a movement that was increasingly identifying with the American South and libertarian elements in the American West. They pushed the postwar conservative mind in a direction that threatened to make it ill-equipped to fit American popular culture. Their arguments were either engorged by the wider movement or swept aside by New Right intellectuals who started to emerge in their wake. Neoconservatives left behind a road not taken, a detour that helped, in the end, cement the conservative identity.[34]

Neoconservatives were high-culture intellectuals who ignored the growing grassroots movement that the *National Review* editors enthused over, retrenching instead to a world of elite writing and magazines. You could see bubbling up within the pages of *Public Interest* (started in 1965) and *Commentary* (which took a turn to the right in 1967 or so) the concerns that would define neoconservatism. In *Public Interest,* writers offered dry articles about community action programs and urban riots as well as increasing poverty and the growing addiction to heroin in the inner city. The writing was measured and balanced. Nathan Glazer, for instance, argued for upgrading low-paying jobs rather than gutting or reforming welfare; Kristol called to reform the welfare state, not abolish it. Nonetheless, neoconservatives unleashed radical ideas even as they quickly stuffed them back into their Pandora's box. When Glazer discussed an "imperial judiciary," a term that would show up again in more extremist conservative writings during the 1990s, he would not condemn the intent of *Brown v. Board of Education* the way *National Review* had but would suggest the court had overreached in trying to pursue a noble goal. When *Public Interest* writers criticized the press, they worried about its power and adversarial tone (especially after Watergate), but there the critique stopped. They did not push into the territory of questioning journalistic objectivity of the "mainstream media" the way other conservative writers had and would in the future. Nonetheless, they put topics on the table of discussion that could go in more radical directions than intended.[35]

Although Russell Kirk might glance slyly at the New Left's rebellion against the multiversity, neoconservatives recoiled. They spoke the language of backlash. The New Left's idea of "participatory democracy" drove neoconservatives particularly nuts, because it generated an "anti-institutional bias." Whereas young YAF'ers might adopt certain New Left protest tactics, *Commentary's* writers saw only a desperate form of existential politics in New Left activism. Student takeovers were temper tantrums substituting for long-term university reform. Neoconservatives believed in rescuing "authority" in the university—an institution they admired for its freedom from political pressures (be those from the Right or Left)—and strengthening administrators against students, without surrendering faculty input. The student demand for "authenticity" against a bureaucratic machine struck these thinkers as silly and dangerous, as did the counterculture project of dropping out of middle-class society. Defending the ideal of university autonomy from politics against the New Left's attempt to politicize the campus pushed neoconservatives to endorse the concept of academic freedom, just the thing that Buckley despised. Nonetheless, neoconservatives kept academe squarely in the sights of the movement even after the 1960s crashed and burned. And as time went on, Kristol himself would argue that the concept of "academic freedom" had become a source of abuse. When he did, it greatly pleased William F. Buckley.[36]

The neoconservatives also kept anti-intellectualism on the map. Here again they added a certain amount of nuance. Take, for instance, the central idea still associated with neoconservative writing of the 1960s and 1970s—the "new class." It was a sociological concept with a great deal of thought behind it, not exactly the same thing as Kirk's or Chambers's doubts about intellectuals. Its central idea was that a class of intellectuals, professionals, and technicians had become more important in a "post-industrial" society where information, knowledge, technology, and science often trumped the power of capital.[37] The idea of a new class dated back to the 1920s, when Thorstein Veblen discovered that "engineers" who worked within the modern corporation battled the short-sighted profit-interests of robber baron capitalists. Before becoming a conservative, James Burnham had written during the 1930s about a "managerial revolution" evident in socialist societies, where "production executives, administrative engineers, supervisory technicians, . . . government bureau heads and commissioners and administrators" assumed high levels of power.[38] The "new class" idea had found a strong home within the mindset of the Left and even liberals like John Kenneth Galbraith, who continued to develop the idea in *The Affluent Society* (1958). For Galbraith, the new class was humane and progressive, concerned with education and the quality of life rather than profit. Daniel Bell rightfully called the term a "muddled concept" with a long history.[39]

The neoconservatives, though, made it a pejorative term—squeezing as much moral juice as they could out of this sociological concept and, in the same breath, making an older, morally infused critique of intellectuals sound updated and social scientific. Kristol emphasized the public and mass media sector of the new class and conveniently overlooked its corporate and managerial wing—concluding that the new class trended leftward in all of its views. In this way, neoconservatives parroted writers at the *National Review* who chastised Galbraith for his positive ruminations about the new class. One reviewer called Galbraith's faith in the new class "ominously reminiscent of Orwell's *1984.*"[40] Neoconservatives were not that different from the Old Right on this point, nor was their criticism of the "new class" all that different from the previous critique of the "liberal establishment" made by Evans. Kristol defined the new class as "an intelligentsia which so despises the ethos of bourgeois society, and which is so guilt-ridden at being implicated in the life of this society." Nothing new there.[41]

Neoconservatives added an air of sophistication to right-wing thinking, but they rarely offered new ideas. More profoundly, they ignored how American political culture had changed by the time they were writing. Consider the issue of religion. In addressing a "crisis in values," neoconservatives offered an old-fashioned solution: a return to religion grounded in a sociological view of faith.[42] Neoconservatives underestimated the fervor of the religious belief they endorsed. Irving Kristol set out the neoconservative view of religion as sociological duty, and in the mid-1990s, he was asked to answer the charge of "hypocrisy," having been a secular Jew who had espoused religious faith. But his later defense only illuminated the original problem. He explained that "more and more Christians and Jews these days who themselves have a secular lifestyle are seeing to it that their children are raised within a religious tradition. Modern secularism has such affinities to moral nihilism that even those who wish simply to affirm or reaffirm moral values have little choice but to seek a grounding for such values in a religious tradition."[43] This might not have been hypocritical, but it sounded utilitarian and refused to note changing realities in American religious culture at the time. Like other neoconservative arguments, the ideas did not match the cultural realities of America, especially not those of the religious-based New Right, including the rising power of evangelical and fundamentalist strains in Christianity.

As historians Maurice Isserman and Michael Kazin point out, "mainstream, mostly white churches" like Episcopalians, Presbyterians, and Methodists shrank in membership during the 1960s and 1970s.[44] The most important long-term growth was in fundamentalist religious sects. The authenticity of evangelicalism—its pure emotionalism and antitheological leanings—won many more souls than mainline Protestant churches (or the odd fascination with Eastern religion that also marked the 1970s). Some fundamentalists might understand their faith's sociological benefits. But that was not the general feel of the "New Christian Right" that arose during the 1970s. Although neoconservatives believed a return to religion could promote collective membership in a wider and more stable national community, the "New Christian Right" nurtured absolutist convictions and even secessionist tendencies—seen most explicitly in the Christian homeschooling movement that began to burgeon during the 1970s. This movement ironically had features similar to the 1960s counterculture—a rebellion that embraced purity and "dropping out" versus collective membership in a pluralist society.[45] The New Right's religious faith was not as bounded as neoconservatives might hope. It did not provide sociological stability, but rather dissent. Neoconservatives wound up talking past the realities of on-the-ground movements.

IRVING KRISTOL'S HAND-WRINGING

Irving Kristol was the most prominent figure in the neoconservative movement. During the 1930s, he was a "neo-Trotskyist";

during the 1950s, a centrist liberal with conservative leanings. In 1952, Kristol discussed "civil liberties" and McCarthyism. He focused attention on liberal critics of Senator McCarthy, like the historian Henry Steele Commager, who he believed had overestimated McCarthy's threat to American democracy. Kristol explained that Americans liked the senator from Wisconsin because he was "unequivocally anti-Communist." "About the spokesmen for American liberalism," he intoned, "they feel they know no such thing. And with some justification."[46] This argument must have warmed the heart of William Buckley, but Kristol shied away from drawing the conclusion others drew from this article—that he was an anticommunist liberal whose anticommunism was stronger than his liberalism.[47] He continued to think of himself as a Cold War liberal as he worked for numerous anticommunist organizations—including the Congress for Cultural Freedom and the British publication, *Encounter*. His anticommunism continued to harden, eventually bleeding into the new conservatism he helped define from the 1960s onward.

As editor of *Public Interest*, Kristol transitioned from Cold War liberal to neoconservative. He edited articles about inner city breakdown and poverty and started to question LBJ's Great Society. He outlined a "conservative welfare state" that would preserve traditional programs like Social Security without promising too much else in the way of social programs. This was not exactly a policy that could get the movement's blood boiling.[48] It was a managerial imperative more than a grassroots call to arms and seemed a return to the middle road that had originally upset conservative intellectuals during the 1950s. For instance, Kristol called for creating "some form of national health insurance" and then criticized the "idiotic hostility to the original Social Security legislation" of the Republican Party.[49] No wonder he hitched his dreams to Nixon. For though Nixon campaigned in 1968 as George Wallace did—defending the "silent majority" against rioters, radical students, and hippies—he governed to the center, even promoting a guaranteed national income, wage and price controls, environmentalist reforms, and extension of the Vietnam War. This was exactly the kind of presidency Kristol could get behind—center right and sometimes liberal. But it was not the future of the conservative movement as a whole, lacking a necessary panache and populist zeal.

Kristol must have chafed at Nixon's campaign language, or so it would seem from his writing about populism. He called populism "an antinomian impulse," a "Jacobin contempt" for "law and order and civility."[50] Populist rhetoric would not work politically for the Right, he warned, because it extolled the producing classes. This view was not grounded in economic or political reality. The populist tradition might have animated the Right—especially Russell Kirk's celebration of petty bourgeois and small town virtues and then George Wallace's and Richard Nixon's political rhetoric—but was becoming increasingly indefensible in postindustrial America, where small producers fell to the power of corporate capitalism. By rejecting populism, though, Kristol did not give up talking about the democratic capacities of ordinary citizens. Instead, he advocated "republican" language (small-r) about the common good and the need for civic virtue. He extolled the ideal of sacrifice captured in the American Revolution.[51]

Unfortunately for Kristol, his political theory of republicanism —with its emphasis on virtue and sacrifice—demanded too much of ordinary citizens. And the populism he derided was, in the simplest of terms, *easier* political theory, because it relied on a circular definition of civic virtue—the people are virtuous because people are virtuous, not because of anything they do, but simply that they are *not* the elite. Kristol's paean to the American Revolution and republican sacrifice sounded dour and demanding. Besides, the American Right was growing more populist by the moment, with even the centrist Nixon talking about the "silent majority" (what did a silent majority need to do but simply vote its true feelings?) and others ranting against the "pointy-headed intellectuals" and liberal elite. Just as the "New Christian Right" did not follow the neoconservatives' version of religion, few followers on the right would find republicanism more appealing than populism.

In all, Kristol was a moralist and handwringer who warned more than he cheered. But warnings could not bolster the movement. This might be one reason why so few of Kristol's writing are read today by conservative intellectuals (and why many of Kristol's books have gone out of print). Though he wrote quite a lot throughout the 1970s (especially op-eds), Kristol became less of an intellectual and more of a networker— helping out the think tank world that would eventually formulate policies for the Reagan Revolution of 1980. Kristol served on corporate boards, held a fellowship at the American Enterprise Institute, and created the Institute for Educational Affairs. As he told Sidney Blumenthal: "I raise money for conservative think tanks. I am a liaison to some degree between intellectuals and the business community."[52] Kristol opened up discussions that others would take in more potent directions. The New Right would harden his critique of the "new class" into populist anti-intellectualism and antiacademic stances. It would do this by throwing overboard his elitism, sophistication, and most certainly his hand-wringing tone.

The Other Face of Neoconservatism: Norman Podhoretz's "New Sensibility"

If Kristol offered one route out of the 1960s that the New Right would bypass, there was yet another face of neoconservatism. Instead of undergoing a 1960s mugging, one neoconservative actually imbibed the decade's "new sensibility." Unlike Kristol, Norman Podhoretz had a close and cozy relationship with what he himself termed the "new radicalism" of the late 1950s and early 1960s. Looking back on a decade that had not quite run its course, he wrote: "I myself have come more and more to see revisionist liberalism," by which Podhoretz meant "Cold War" liberalism, "as involving an abdication of the intellectual's proper role as a critic of society." Podhoretz seemed to elbow his way into the "adversary culture" of the "new class" only to elbow himself out of it into neoconservative ranks. Disgruntled with liberalism, he drifted left during the late 1950s and early 1960s, even though his lifestyle reflected the stereotype of the "silent generation." He had married early and adopted children in the process and then landed a successful job as an editor in his twenties.[53] And yet, he seemed to chafe at this early self-enforced adulthood. Writing in 1957 about the "Young Generation," he pointed out in terms that sounded autobiographical (as would all his writing): "Since this is a generation that willed itself from childhood directly into adulthood, it still has its adolescence to go through—for a man can never skip adolescence, he can only postpone it. And something very wonderful may come about when a whole generation in its late thirties breaks loose and decides to take a swim in the Plaza fountain in the middle of the night." Podhoretz would publish some of those swimmers— including thinkers who would influence the New Left—and sometimes take a swim himself.[54]

This might seem surprising considering that Podhoretz was known for his famous takedown of the Beat writers—the same ones that Evans and Buckley admitted liking. For Podhoretz, the "Know-Nothing Bohemians" of the Beat movement—Kerouac and Ginsberg—worshipped "primitivism, instinct, energy, 'blood.' " Sounding like Kristol, Podhoretz condemned the Beats' "anti-intellectualism" and "populistic" sensibilities.[55] He foresaw Paul Goodman, who criticized the Beats for being "inarticulate" and posing no threat to the "organized society" they impishly criticized.[56] But this did not mean Podhoretz was divorced from the "new sensibility," far from it. What Podhoretz

doubted about the Beats, he more than made up for in his love
of Norman Mailer—a more serious writer and thinker, as far as
Podhoretz was concerned, and one who was clearly on the Left
but whose 1960s *style* would wind up offering potent conservative possibilities.

Podhoretz formed a friendship with Mailer that was
"intense."[57] But it was not based on politics. After all, Mailer was
a Popular Front holdover who endorsed Henry Wallace for president in 1948 and then developed an odd, anarchist, left-wing
politics that Podhoretz never saw much worth in. What mattered
was Mailer's conception of intellectual life, best exhibited in his
collected set of essays, *Advertisements for Myself* (1959). Central to
the book was Mailer's famous piece on the hipster, "The White
Negro," which celebrated violence and a short-term quest for
kicks, the perfect expression of left-wing, apocalyptic, and
nihilist thought. Podhoretz seemed to fixate instead on Mailer's
ponderings about being a self-publicizing, self-obsessed writer
who talked about himself no matter the subject. He learned
from Mailer's discovery that publicity and the self-induced narcissism of celebrity mattered more than intellectual argument.
Generating a persona and projecting it outward became crucial in
America's consumer culture. Mailer explained: "To write about
myself is to send my style through a circus of variations and pos-
tures, a fireworks of virtuosity designed to achieve . . . I do not
even know what." It would at least achieve publicity. Mailer
would sometimes refer to himself as the "general," suggesting he
was mapping out a war against his enemies as he wrote in bold
and sweeping terms about subject matters that required a bit
more attention than he was willing to pay. He went for shock
and controversy more than analysis or argument. He could say, in
his ponderings about the hipster, that "the act of rape" could
have "artistry" (this from a man who would eventually stab
his wife). Mailer wanted his book's pages to show him as a
manly antihero chafing at the limits of middle-class sensibility,

as rebellion personified. And his own existential hipsterism hoped to transcend the dull politics of liberalism—the same liberalism Podhoretz was chafing at. For Mailer, liberalism lacked feeling and excitement, having become an ideology of the well-fed and complacent.[58]

When Podhoretz started moving to the right, he took Mailer's techniques with him—especially hipness and self-confession. For Podhoretz, the best writing was autobiographical, providing details of the writer's life, confessing as much as arguing. Again, this made clear Podhoretz's indebtedness to the "new sensibility" of the time—not just Mailer but the wider movement of "new journalism" that included Hunter S. Thompson and Joan Didion. Podhoretz hit on his future style in "My Negro Problem" (1963), where he reflected on his own experience of being bullied by black kids in his neighborhood. This autobiographical detail explained why some Jews might be hesitant about allying with African Americans in their contemporary struggles for equality. *Take my own feelings seriously,* Podhoretz demanded of his readers. Honesty was as important an intellectual tactic as detached analysis, confession as important as historical reasoning. And so Podhoretz was finding ways to merge the "new sensibility" of the 1960s with what could become conservative ideas. He suggested: *I'm not sure I like black people and am not sure all their demands should be met—but, hey, I'm just a hung-up, normal white guy who got bullied and decided to write openly about it.* He documented his fear and even his "hatred," suggesting that hypocritical white liberals would never have the guts to do this. He expressed his doubts about integration and intermarriage (even if he begrudgingly accepted such things). In writing personal confessions, he offered a path that could take him down a very conservative—yet ultimately hipper—road.[59]

Podhoretz made a career of gossiping about himself and his fellow intellectuals. His most famous and accomplished books center on pissing off his friends and then telling about pissing off his friends—*Making It* and then *Breaking Ranks* and more recently *Ex-Friends*.[60] Podhoretz found a way to take it to the intellectuals—to slam the "new class"—but with much more style, sexiness, and panache than Kristol's sermonizing. *Making It* was a transitional book and one that his friends, including Mailer, warned him against publishing. Podhoretz called it a "confessional work." His message was this: *We intellectuals are just like you common readers, with your ambitions, hang-ups, and obsessions.* Mailer had already pursued this in *Advertisements for Myself,* illustrating the nervousness of the writer and the desire to promote himself and get heard, all of which seemed motivated by baser ambitions than literary artistry. For Podhoretz, confession could fire up anti-intellectualism. There's a "connection between the study of literature and the contempt for success," he explained, sounding an awful lot like Kristol moaning about the new class's hatred of "bourgeois" society. But he debunked the intellectual "contempt for success" by discussing his own excitement at being accepted into the circle of the New York intellectuals, by becoming part of the *Commentary* office, and by getting drunk at *Partisan Review* parties. Telling these stories told something more: *Yes, I'm a writer and seemingly aspire for ideals and truth, but really I share with all of you "narcissism" and a desire for material "success."* He underscored the point: "literary intellectuals are no different from other mortals." Anti-intellectualism found new expression in the figure of the self-lacerating writer.[61]

The book was catharsis and a way to mimic Mailer. "For several years I toyed with the idea of doing a book about Mailer that would focus on the problem of success," he explained at the end of *Making It.* The book he conceived would have to be "in the first person" and "frank" and about "distinction, fame, and money" and about the literary world's "dirty little secret." Instead, he wrote *Making It,* and the book succeeded by making him "the main topic of conversations at dinner parties in New York." By 1973, Podhoretz was openly deriding the "bigoted attitudes toward the general American populace which have become so widespread within the intellectual community." But this general argument against intellectuals that littered neoconservative writings had already been developed in his autobiographical ponderings. Because writers and intellectuals, including Norman Mailer, criticized *Making It,* Podhoretz felt "betrayed by the literary world." But no matter, as that only confirmed his growing sense that intellectuals were hypocritical snobs. And so, the "new sensibility"—the insistent sense of writing as a therapeutic act of self-confession—became a way to justify the "new conservatism." Attacking the "new class" could also serve as literary high jinks and fun—the comical touch lent by the "anti-intellectualism of the intellectuals"—and could sell books the way sermonizing never could. It fit the confessional mode that would become more prominent in American culture and that the 1960s helped nurture.[62]

Podhoretz's autobiographical critique of the new class wedded itself to his growing concern about American foreign policy after Vietnam. He felt responsible to address the resulting malaise left behind by the Vietnam quagmire—that growing doubt that America could manage to do good in the world. The enemy on this front was a cultural *feeling,* especially apparent among academics and intellectuals (the new class). It was a loss of "American confidence in American power." Podhoretz made what was lost sound almost magical: "Anything within reason we wanted to do we believed we had the power to do." That feeling was destroyed by Vietnam, Podhoretz argued, a war that left behind only "pacifism, anti-Americanism, and isolationism" in its wake. And it is here that the "neoconservative," as we presently understand the figure today, emerges, in a reassertion of American power abroad and a toughness that opposes the "culture of appeasement" espoused by "new liberal isolationists" at home. Podhoretz railed against the "détente" practiced by Nixon, Ford, and Carter. And he offered a potent vision of

American power that would emerge in Reagan's presidency and George W. Bush's policy in Iraq.[63]

But what mattered most was the way Podhoretz offered his critique. This was not Kristol's moralizing criticism. Instead of sermonizing, Podhoretz talked about his own feelings and perceptions of his literary circles and then relished in the good aura of previous foreign policy initiatives of the United States. His was an attitude of the present harkening back to the past. Podhoretz had cut his teeth on the "new sensibility" of the 1960s. He was *of* the decade in ways that Kristol could never be. Yes, Podhoretz bashed liberals and the new class, but he did so in a way that had a 1960s flair to it. He did not warn conservatives about the dangers of liberalism or populism as much as he talked about himself and celebrated the possibilities of American power abroad. In his career the postwar conservative mind could see at least a part of its future—a more promising future than that promised by Irving Kristol's moral hand-wringing.

FROM NEOCONSERVATIVES TO NEW RIGHT

The neoconservatives were not the only and certainly not the most important development on the Right in the wake of the 1960s. After all, Russell Kirk and some others followed out the logic of rebellion to its rightful conclusion: that the critique of the bureaucratic university could ally (partially) with New Left rebellion. At the same time, William Buckley celebrated the grassroots activism of right-wing students and Goldwater's campaign as sources for a new configuration in American politics—a grassroots activism that shared quite a bit with the New Left. By the late 1960s, though, a newer form of right-wing populism had come into full swing. It was most visible in George Wallace who "had begun" by 1967, as his biographer points out, "to blend the themes of the religious right into a message emphasizing the threat posed to American traditions and values, by the national state and the 'liberal elite' that dominated American society." This vision for politics (taken up in Nixon's "silent majority" rhetoric and southern strategy) held the future roadmap for the Right. Unlike the neoconservative detour into republican virtue, this populist style went back to the Old Right's love of Joseph McCarthy and the "massive resistance" against the civil rights movement. The New Right treated the neoconservative interruption as just that—a moment of doubt and hesitation necessary to be transcended. Populist confidence had stuck in the cortex of the conservative mind, no matter how hard Kristol hoped to push it out.[64]

Nixon had a court-intellectual, Kevin Phillips, who developed the New Right idea perfectly, tracing out its bold populist contours. He differed from both neoconservatives and the *National Review* crowd. His political role model was Wallace himself, who had shown better than Nixon how backlash against the civil rights and the anti-Vietnam movements created new political possibilities. Phillips developed a theory of conservative populism based on polls, historical voting patterns, and demographics. Whereas the *National Review* set and the neoconservatives loved to discuss political philosophy, Phillips evaded abstract political theory for analyzing how population growth and demographic patterns played out politically. *The Emerging Republican Majority* (1969), his first and most important book, read like a set of charts, statistics, and maps. The conclusion, though, was drawn explicitly in a 1971 op-ed piece in which Phillips embraced "the forgotten whites" who were "tired of hearing upper-crust talk about equal justice for blacks while there remains no chance" that there would be "a Polish president of General Motors." His was a politics for alienated whites and "smalltown America," a populist alternative to Kristol's hand-wringing.[65]

Phillips's opposition to the neoconservatives can be gleaned from the pages of *The New Class?*, a book of essays released in

1979 and edited by B. Bruce-Briggs, an urban planner and historian. Bruce-Briggs included essays by the democratic socialist Michael Harrington and Norman Podhoretz (whose essay was unimaginatively titled "The Adversary Culture and the New Class"). Though the book featured neoconservatives prominently, its sharpest essay, in political terms, was Phillips's. The concept of the new class for Phillips was not sociological or moral but explicitly political. Phillips called George Wallace "the first politician in the United States to respond directly to the impact of the New Class." He then spelled out a distinction between "neoconservative" reactions to the new class and the New Right's. "The 'New Right' represents a very different and much less fashionable set of forces. While neo-conservatives harass the New Class in magazine articles and intellectual discourse, but lack a mass constituency and make little effort to defeat New Class politicians and programs, the New Right is essentially nonintellectual and deals in populist mobilization of grassroots lower-middle and middle-class constituencies on issues like abortion, busing, education, textbooks, school prayer, the Panama Canal, and property taxes." Phillips was comfortable with this "non" (anti?) "intellectualism." He saw it as an essential tool for winning political power. That is, the concept of the new class served not just as a category to sermonize about, but as a political weapon. Phillips rejected Kristol's hand-wringings about populism and endorsed not the neoconservatives but the "New Right"—a term he helped push into American political discussion at the time.[66]

At first, neoconservative intellectuals attacked the ponderings of Phillips and other "New Right" intellectuals. In 1977, for instance, Jeane Kirkpatrick, eventually the U.S. ambassador to the United Nations under Ronald Reagan but then still a Democrat who tended toward neoconservatism, thrashed Kevin Phillips (as well as Patrick Buchanan and Richard Whalen) in the pages of *Commentary*. These New Rightists ignored that the

American populace was not *that* conservative. The Wallace-ite Right and McGovernish Left alienated too many people, so conservatives needed to move to the center and criticize the "strain of native populism" within the New Right.[67] Many neoconservative centrists concurred. Nathan Glazer, though never a full-fledged neoconservative but a dancer on the movement's edges, completely disassociated himself from strident right-wing thinking owing to his "less energetic social style"—a telling phrase indeed. Stridency was a turn-off, and overpoliticizing the new class was dangerous, or at least it seemed to the neoconservatives who did not have the stomach for the more combative conservative style of the New and now the Old Right. The neoconservatives had to put up or shut up—either get with the more strident feel of the movement or play the role of worrying, hand-wringing, sideline-standing naysayers. The neoconservative view of religion failed the New Right, as did the warning made against the dangers of populism.[68]

Neoconservatives offered a thoughtful critique of the movement they wanted to join, but they did not have as much room to maneuver. Recall here how Kristol's own critique of leftist academics started centrist but moved rightward. This was a metaphor for the neoconservative movement as a whole. When it could not fit the realities of the conservative movement or the pressures of America's political culture, the neoconservatives moved right. The journalist Damon Linker argues that "by the mid-1980s" neoconservative figures like Podhoretz and Kristol had "come to share the conviction that a religious-populist insurgency on the part of the American people would make it possible to retake cultural territory lost since the 1960s"—a remarkable move considering the roots of neoconservative thought.[69] Nonetheless, neoconservative suspicion about populism remained behind, and when some "theocons" and New Rightists called for civil disobedience against the American judiciary during the mid-1990s, thinkers like Podhoretz bolted.

He explained that he "did not become a conservative in order to become a radical" and that theocons in endorsing civil disobedience, seemed like "left wing radicals of the 1960s."[70] Podhoretz could only go part of the way with the populism inherent in the "new sensibility." Thus, neoconservatives either had to face their limits and merge with the wider movement or jump ship.

But that's getting ahead of our story. What is important to recognize is that by the 1970s, there were two important strains that the conservative mind could ingest and work with. The first was the "new sensibility" found in Podhoretz's writing. The other was George Wallace's populist anger and Phillips's arguments on its behalf—both which clashed against the more respectable republicanism of Kristol. The conservative mind had to marry these two strains, to make the "new sensibility" cohabitate with populism. Some conservative intellectuals recognized there was something genuinely "American" about the sixties—about the decade's authenticity, rebellion, and raucous democracy—no matter what neoconservatives like Kristol might worry about. There seemed the possibility of jettisoning the liberalism of the 1960s while holding on to the decade's utopianism, radicalism, cultural rebellion, and populism. The 1960s had left its mark on the conservative intellectual movement, and the conservative intellectual movement had left its own mark on the decade. And out of that would be born the postmodern conservative mind. The neoconservatives exerted a last push for a project that could never take root in America—an elitist conservatism that eschewed populism, democracy, and raucousness. Those elements of their hopes could not be sustained. They yielded, as they had to, and contributed to the final chapter in the making of the conservative mind.

THREE

Postmodern Conservatism, the Politics of Outrage, and the Mindset of War

In political warfare you do not fight just to prevail in an argument, but to destroy the enemy's fighting ability. Republicans often seem to regard political combats as they would a debate with the Oxford Political Union, as though winning depended on rational arguments and carefully articulated principles. But the audience of politics is not made up of Oxford dons, and the rules are entirely different. . . . Politics is war. Don't forget it. —David Horowitz, 2000

IT WAS OCTOBER 1987. Ronald Reagan had been elected president twice, and the utopian dreams of the Left and the counterculture of the 1960s flickered like ghosts from the past. The Right had won just rewards in a presidency that came close to matching its views (Reagan had cut his political teeth within the Goldwater campaign of 1964). Still, those assembled in a conference room in downtown Washington, D.C., just could not get over the 1960s or the New Left. They called their event the "Second Thoughts" conference. The idea was to have those who were once radical leftists during the 1960s confess errors and reconsider their political ideas. They would confab with an older generation of neoconservatives and strengthen the conservative intellectual movement in the process.

When David Horowitz appeared at the dais, he was, by one description, "clad in retro-Berkeley style: tight, stone-washed jeans; black lizard-skin boots; and white T-shirt emblazoned, 'Nicaragua is Spanish for Afghanistan.'" Some believed him to be the 1980s equivalent of Whittaker Chambers, having shed his 1960s radicalism for 1980s conservatism. And to a certain extent, the comparison made sense. Chambers had replaced his communism with a new ideology just as absolutist. Horowitz did the same, and he too hung on to tactics learned during his radical left-wing past (as did Chambers when he purged Ayn Rand). From his days in the 1960s, Horowitz carried forth a style of political combativeness nurtured during his time at *Ramparts* magazine and the Black Panther Party. He loved not just the sixties "look" projected at the dais but the sixties spirit of confrontationalism and hardball politics. As much as the ends changed—moving from left to right—the means remained the same.[1]

Some of the more elderly neoconservatives assembled started to chafe at the tones of the conference. They worried that the 1960s radicalism was not being shed at all, that the decade that mugged them had not been treated in the full sense of its criminality. The legacy of Irving Kristol's moralism and hand-wringing could be heard among some conference participants. Art critic and neoconservative Hilton Kramer, for instance, mounted the podium and berated the younger generation: "Not a single mention of the counterculture," he boomed. "Well, you were all immoralists. And we are all paying the price for the agenda let loose." To a large extent, Kramer was right. Horowitz, the prime organizer of the conference and its key spokesperson, had not dumped his 1960s style or political ethic any more than Norman Podhoretz had dumped the decade's "new sensibility" as he marched into the future. The 1960s had become a permanent fixture of Horowitz's identity, as it had for the country as a whole. Horowitz was the sixties hipster marching in line with the "Reagan Revolution," and he determined the future of the conservative intellectual movement more than Kramer's or Kristol's anguished, highbrow concern.[2]

Horowitz is an exemplar of the postmodern conservative intellectual. The figure appears new, as if born only after the 1960s. But the postmodern conservative intellectual is also a pastiche of inheritances from the post–World War II past as a whole. There was the residual rebel stance of 1950s conservatives— the sense of being tough-ass outsiders like Buckley crashing the gates of Yale's ivy walls. The postmodern conservative embraced the status of permanent rebel against a liberal establishment, even though that liberal establishment was rather rickety by that point. There was the legacy of Podhoretz's "new sensibility," the personalizing of political beliefs and the projection of conservative hipsterism. There was also the New Right's populist disdain for elitism and intellectualism, now bolstered by academic theories about the indeterminacy of truth and the liberatory powers of popular culture. And most obviously, there was the confrontational style bequeathed by the 1960s. Horowitz inherited all of these strains, especially the last.

Horowitz certainly had "second thoughts" about the sixties, but he never really got over the decade. After all, it taught him too much. Horowitz approvingly quoted the cultural critic Camille Paglia who described him as "the true 1960s spirit— audacious and irreverent, yet passionately engaged and committed to social change."[3] Never a truer statement has been made, for in fighting the culture wars by writing numerous autobiographies about how he shed his sixties radicalism (an inheritance of the 1960s "new sensibility" and its exaltation of the self's confessions), arguing that slavery benefited African Americans, and sponsoring a Student Bill of Rights that would have state legislatures police classrooms for purported liberal content, Horowitz turned lessons learned from the 1960s into a conservative strategy of attack. In *The Art of Political War*, a small book that then–House Speaker Tom DeLay once distributed to numerous Republican congressmen, Horowitz drew up a playbook for roughness akin to the confrontational student protests of the 1960s. "Aggression is advantageous," Horowitz wrote, "because politics is a war of position." Republicans needed to take up the "cause of the underdog" and retool themselves as waging war against privilege. In other words, the Right had to appropriate the language of the Left and use it to slam back and win power. It must become, as Whittaker Chambers had argued for conservative Cold War battles, just as tough as the *other* side.[4]

Ironically, Horowitz made the point best while seeming to shed his sixties radicalism. He performed a juggling act, where the 1960s style remained and 1960s ideas were attacked. In *Destructive Generation: Second Thoughts about the Sixties*, a book cowritten with Peter Collier, Horowitz documented the zaniness of the late 1960s Left, especially the break-up of SDS into fanatical factions including the Weather Underground. He documented the thugishness of the Black Panther Party and Tom Hayden's flirtation with revolutionary terrorism. Some of the book seems remorseful, but its more strident message becomes explicit in an anecdote told at its end. There the authors discuss a confrontation with the cultural guru of the 1960s, Susan Sontag. They did not deride her for her celebration of "camp" over high culture or her attack on "interpretation" as a violation of art's surfaces—all arguments made during the 1960s that are now part and parcel of what we could call postmodernism (and most likely what would have driven Hilton Kramer nuts about her work). Indeed, Horowitz would actually use Sontag's postmodern language in many of his future battles. What drove Horowitz and Collier crazy about Sontag was that she never renounced her radical political stances from the past. They asked her why she had allowed a 1969 essay celebrating the Viet Cong to be republished in a recent anthology. Sontag chafed and said: "I don't want to enter your world, where you push every-thing to extremes." Their response to the charge was telling: "We realized she was right—we did push things to extremes." In other words, as much as things changed, they stayed the same.[5]

THE POSTMODERN TURN IN CONSERVATIVE THOUGHT

Horowitz sees himself as a rebel today as much as he was in the 1960s. And he shares the same enemy conservatives chastised in the past—the "liberal establishment." Though postmodern con-servative intellectuals faced a liberal establishment more weak than in the 1950s, they focused on the same institutions, espe-cially the modern university and the liberal media. There were new enemies, of course, like President Bill Clinton—a politician who focused conservative ire in ways bordering on the obsessive—and feminists. But much remained from the past as conservatives crossed the cultural divide into postmodernity and made their own important contributions to its zeitgeist. The times and younger audiences demanded that any remaining element of fuddy-duddy style be purged from the conservative mind. The times also offered a way to make old arguments sound new and acquire more credibility.

Though a slippery term, "postmodernism" can be defined first and foremost as a long-term exhaustion of modern rationalism. The cultural historian Morris Dickstein once connected this strain of postmodernity to the 1960s: "One of the healthier things we learned in the sixties, and are unlikely to forget, was to be more skeptical of the pose of objectivity." Distrust about the claims of powerful actors who used tones of rationality, disinterestedness, and objectivity lasted long after debates surrounding the Vietnam War (they are nicely captured in shots of Defense Secretary Robert McNamara displaying charts and graphs to justify troop escalation in Vietnam, shown evocatively in Errol Morris's documentary, *The Fog of War*). Rationality itself started to look irrational—this was a

central feature of so much 1960s protest and political criticism discussed in numerous places, including the *Intercollegiate Review*.
Writers like Theodore Roszak believed that the decade's "counterculture" radicalized the idea as it grew disillusioned with "the conventional scientific world view" and "man's infatuation with the
machine." The counterculture's expressive individualism pushed
aside McNamara's cold-hearted scientific outlook and conjured a
"non-intellective consciousness" through drugs, rock music, and, of
course, the "new sensibility" of the time.[6]

"Tenured radicals," the term used for radical leftists then
finding warm solace in 1980s academe, carried much of the
1960s spirit into the halls with them. Critiques of "logocentrism" and universal claims to truth became the intellectual tools
of the academic Left (most prominently visible in literary and
aesthetic theory). Consider Susan Sontag's critique of "interpretation" as an act of violation of art's visual erotics, Richard Rorty's
and Jacques Derrida's "antifoundationalism," Jean-François Lyotard's
dissection of "metanarratives," or Stanley Fish's rejection of "objective" meaning and an embrace of individual reception of texts.
All these arguments questioned the universal foundations for
Western truth-claims. Postmodernism exploded the universalis-
tic pretensions of the West (for instance, the language of "rights"
and "reason") as too tightly bound up with domination and
power, especially when placed in the context of the West's colo-
nial domination of the non-Western world. Universalism, one
philosopher explained in a long work that tried to define the
term "postmodernism," is "now seen as an anxious and pretentious and yet ultimately futile effort to enforce rigor and unifor-
mity in an unruly world." Thus, "universalism has been replaced
by eclecticism and pluralism." By embracing these ideas, the academic Left threw off its own intellectual inheritances. As the historian John Patrick Diggins once quipped: "The Academic Left
was the first Left in American history to distrust the eighteenth-
century Enlightenment."[7]

The postmodern turn generated suspicions about intellectuals' role in public life. This was particularly evident in Europe, where there was once a great deal of respect paid to intellectuals and where poststructuralism made its first splash. As the intellectual historian Mark Lilla put it: "The days" in Europe "when intellectuals turned to philosophers to get their political bearings, and the public turned to intellectuals, are all but over."[8] During the 1960s and 1970s, Michel Foucault rebelled against his elder, Jean-Paul Sartre, who spoke in utopian and universal language but who wound up apologizing for Soviet totalitarianism. The idea of critics standing outside and passing universal and objective judgment on their society's injustices was no longer defensible, especially as truth-claims appeared culturally and historically bound. Foucault himself, we now know, showed a frightening sympathy for the Iranian revolutionists who, in 1979, threw off the Western prejudices of the shah for Islamic fundamentalism. For Foucault, the universal project of the Enlightenment associated with the West had exhausted itself, and "the 'universal' intellectual" was now dead. Instead, Foucault endorsed the "specific" intellectual serving as a mouthpiece for voiceless groups.[9]

What do these developments usually associated with poststructuralism and the academic Left have to do with the conservative intellectual movement? A great deal. Recall William F. Buckley's attack on the Yale professoriate's pretentious claims to academic freedom. By the 1970s, this anti-intellectual strain grew more explicit. The New Right activist Paul Weyrich argued that "the Old Right was strong on intellectualism," pointing his finger at the *National Review* crowd. For Weyrich, the "intellectualization of conservatism" limited the movement's impact.[10] He echoed Kevin Phillips's celebration of George Wallace's attack on "pointy-headed intellectuals." Though neoconservatives might have appeared as the Right's last gasp of high intellectualism, Kristol's condemnation of an overeducated new class and Podhoretz's personal diminution of intellectuals in his autobiographical reflections suggest otherwise. The intellectual, in all of these treatments, appears not only snobbish and self-important but self-interested, certainly undeserving of pronouncing truths that transcend the faiths and beliefs of ordinary citizens. In other words, conservatives had gotten to Foucault's position much easier and often much earlier.[11]

This feature of postmodern conservatism, strange as it might sound at first, helps explain the rise of one of the more prominent new groupings among right-wing intellectuals—the "theocons" who rose to prominence during the 1990s and published their writings in the pages of *First Things*. These thinkers spoke directly from their religious faith and rejected the need to translate their ideas into a more universal language or separate them from their Catholic roots. Neoconservatives might have touted the virtues of religious belief, but it was from a rationalistic perspective (that is, the sociological payoff or benefit of belief). Writers like Richard John Neuhaus, George Weigel, and Michael Novak, in contrast, criticized American public policy from the standpoint of papal declarations and even went so far as to declare the legitimacy of civil disobedience against a corrupt judiciary in the name of Catholic moral principles. Theocons built on the New Right of the late 1970s, especially Jerry Falwell, the Moral Majority, and Christian Voice, that had already displaced the more secular language of Barry Goldwater. The terms of the Enlightenment became for theocons simply an impediment to faith, little else. Witnessing 9/11, they called for "Christian America" to battle "militant Islam," making their religious particularism more explicit and reaching back to the religious war metaphor used by Whittaker Chambers during the Cold War. Theocons might appear a logical extension of Chambers's thinking, but their prominence also represents a postmodern imperative to find alternatives to Enlightenment rationalism. Religious particularism matched the era better than neoconservative secularism, offering a merger of absolutist faith with relativistic ramifications.[12]

This brings us to the final feature of postmodern culture worthy of discussion: cultural fragmentation. Again, this development is traditionally associated with the academic Left—especially the rise of multiculturalism and "identity politics" in the wake of the black power and feminist movements of the 1960s.[13] Faith in a unified culture trumping disparate identities grew tentative after the battles of the 1960s exposed racial oppression and gender disparities; the 1970s emphasis on "black is beautiful" and ethnic pride only pushed the envelope further. The resulting feel of postmodernity is largely a sense of fracturing and splitting apart, of pluralistic identities breaking up any overarching sense of collective belonging. Though conservatives are traditionally known as critics of identity politics and multiculturalism, they have contributed to cultural fragmentation in increasingly louder tones.

The clearest indication is the vituperative style that defines conservative writing today—its highly charged rhetoric and shrillness evident to any casual observer. Prominent conservative intellectuals do not conceptualize their role as engaging a wider public through civilized debate. Instead, they act as cheerleaders for their side's belief system, reconfirming entrenched opinions among the already-believing and preaching to the choir. Their writing style mirrors the advice given to politicians by Karl Rove, the Republican Party's political mastermind who argued that conservatives should play to their "base," building a politics out of pillorying the enemy and winning victories through small margins. In a society that fragments political opinions and associates those opinions with "lifestyles" of red versus blue states (NASCAR-loving conservatives versus latte-drinking liberals), conservative intellectuals feel obliged to stoke the anger of their own segmented audience. Thus, the histrionic tenor of writers like Ann Coulter and Michael Savage—two of the

Right's best-selling authors. Their books serve as the finest expressions of how postmodern conservative intellectual life contributes to and is informed by cultural fragmentation.[14]

Ann Coulter has accrued the most fame (through intellectual "branding")—more than any other conservative writer. She clearly inherits Buckley's 1950s penchant for shock and "vaudeville." She has cultivated a persona of venom and meanness that sells large quantities of books. But nobody reads her books to learn anything they did not already know. The tone is of red-faced shouting and screaming—not the sort of style that prompts people to reconsider their opinions. For instance, liberals are not just wrong for Coulter, they are demonic. "If Americans knew" what liberals "really believed," she writes, "the public would boil them in oil." For Coulter, "liberals are like Arabs without the fighting spirit." It is better to throttle them (to make a "war of aggression," as David Horowitz called it). As Coulter put it in her book *How to Talk to a Liberal (if You Must)*—that parenthetical portion of the title evokes her thesis—the way to argue is this: "You must outrage the enemy. If the liberal you're arguing with doesn't become speechless with sputtering, impotent rage, you're not doing it right." Coulter plays well to an audience that wants to secede from a wider public sphere—nurturing a conservative fan club that holds its opinions in airtight vacuums and disengages from the demands of civilized discourse, leaving its enemies "sputtering" with "rage."[15]

Alongside Ann Coulter stands Michael Savage, a man who acquired fame in the world of talk radio, not exactly known as an intellectually sophisticated medium. Savage is especially interesting, because his biography highlights another postmodern theme: that the postmodern self lacks coherence and is simply a series of different poses that rely on social confirmation or media affirmation. Consider Savage's life story: born Michael Alan Weiner more than sixty-five years ago, he became a hippie who once "swam naked with Allen Ginsberg" and got "married in a rain forest and studied ethno-medicine at the University of California at Berkeley." During the 1970s, he hung out at City Lights Bookstore, the capital of Beatnik culture, and wrote about herbal medicine and health food. He then became a small capitalist, marketing herbal supplements and teas. Then as the country drifted rightward, he decided to become a talk show host of "The Savage Nation," where he calls for nuking the Middle East, shooting illegal immigrants, and taking out "commies, pinkos, and perverts."[16]

Savage's books read like the rants of a talk radio show host whose bellowing is matched by his audience's frantic nodding and cheering. Liberalism for him, as it is for Coulter, is a "mental disorder" that has "so twisted reality" that "the terrorists are tolerated when they should be annihilated" and that glorifies "Arafat, Kinsey, and Clinton . . . when they should be vilified." Savage moves with blistering speed from one opinion to another, failing to check if they make sense together. For instance, he condemns liberals for a "godless worldview" and then quickly leaps into a treatment of the rock singer Madonna "and the Kabala," as if his own mind's instantaneous connection should be obvious to all. His books become a group of incoherent thoughts that only those already convinced might find convincing. They succeed (at least in terms of sales) owing to the postmodern currents into which they play, preaching to the segmented choir. And they point to a general rise in what some call "smashmouth" commentary that has defined the Right.[17]

The Happier and Hipper Side: The *Weekly Standard*'s Cultural Populism

It would be wrong to reduce the world of postmodern conservatism to the bomb-throwing polemics of Coulter and Savage. The conservative mind would not have won the respect it has if it had not reached out further. That explains another side to the postmodern turn in conservative thought, one that is friendlier though just as populist. It is evident at the *Weekly Standard*, a magazine founded in 1995 that started to push aside the *National Review* by projecting an image of youth, freshness, and intellectual prowess. Its editors openly worried about conservatives being tagged as closed-minded theocons or hard-ass Coulter-types. They moved comfortably into a new postmodern era armed with a hipper and less hysterical demeanor. They attack liberals too, just with a cooler style.

The *Weekly Standard* pioneered a style of hip, conservative populism. Two key founding editors were John Podhoretz, the son of Norman Podhoretz, and William (Bill) Kristol, son of Irving Kristol. Sometimes called "mini-cons," these younger conservative writers took advantage of their fathers' legacies (and names) while pushing in new directions, succeeding, for instance, in the world of cable television. Podhoretz, who would leave the *Standard* after just a few years, had started his career at the *Washington Times*, where he wrote about popular culture. "No subject was too trivial to share with readers," one journalist explains. "Topics included his trip to an amusement park; his hatred of household pets; his love of Jell-O; conversations with an imaginary friend." He also wrote a lot about television sitcoms. He shed any remnant of his father's seriousness, plumbing the recesses of pop culture in order to be "cool and reactionary" at the same time. It is hard to imagine the elder Podhoretz writing about television sitcoms, but then again the son's pop culture obsession seems a logical outgrowth of his father's "new sensibility."[18]

Podhoretz's work at the *Washington Times* reflected a wider trend in postmodern intellectual life typically associated with the academic Left—the growing influence of "cultural studies" and pop culture populism. Sometime during the 1990s, the academic Left rejected its intellectual inheritance from those first-generation academic Marxists known as the Frankfurt School, especially the elitism implicit in the work of Theodor

Adorno and Max Horkheimer. Remembering the power of Hitler's propaganda, these German expatriates dissected the "culture industry" of advanced capitalist societies, emphasizing the influence of culture as much as the economic forces of production. Theodor Adorno, for instance, studied popular songs played on American radio and believed they lolled listeners into a passive state, inducing a "childish" love of liking the same song over and over and becoming "forcibly retarded" and "infantile." Adorno ridiculed the popular dance known as "the jitterbug" as a sign of people's capacity to "affirm and mock their loss of individuality." He believed only the difficult and challenging work of the composer Arnold Schönberg—its "dissonance" rejecting the "illusion of existing harmony"—and other works of high culture could provide a robust alternative to the culture industry's manipulation. Adorno, like his American counterpart Dwight Macdonald, wore his elitism proudly on his sleeve. High culture offered the only resistance to the phoniness of kitsch.[19]

During the 1980s and 1990s, academic leftists in cultural studies programs bristled at Adorno's elitism and insisted that consumers were not dupes. They eschewed theories of cultural manipulation, speaking instead of "empowerment" and the ability of consumers to elide the control of corporate marketeers. The academic Left became cultural populists. Constance Penley, a leading figure in cultural studies "best known for her work on pornographic fanzines in which the *Star Trek* characters get it on," has argued, "All viewers or consumers have 'agency'; they process what they see or hear—they do not merely lap it up." The English professor and now theorist of advertising, James Twitchell, once pointed out: "Watching television is almost frantic with creative activity." Ordinary citizens held power, and what they professed to like—be it television shows or popular music—deserved serious treatment by intellectuals. Academic critics could no longer focus on highbrow literature; they needed to watch *Star Trek* reruns or load up their iPods or "learn from Las Vegas." The populist persuasion in cultural studies demanded such.[20]

Podhoretz agreed with his compatriots on the Left. Pop culture and its promise of democratic enjoyment enthused him. And his interest carried over into the magazine he helped edit. Flip through the *Weekly Standard* during the 1990s, and you find numerous stories about popular culture: football, television shows, celebrities, even professional wrestling. This is one reason why some leftists found the magazine more interesting than their own humdrum political journals. Writing about popular culture made the editors seem cool, testifying that conservative intellectuals, if they worried about the matter, were no longer stuck-up prigs but rather *South Park* devotees and "hipublicans." They knew were where the action was.[21]

Podhoretz's cultural populism also fit the prosperous, go-go 1990s, when large numbers of Republicans flocked to Washington, D.C. His was a populism of SUV's and television sports—a populism for a new upper middle class living inside the beltway, especially the suburbs of Virginia and Maryland. The *Weekly Standard* pledged to speak for a people's way of life against elitist attack. In typical fashion, Fred Barnes could write an article that fawned about the new suburban culture: "I like highways, the more lanes, the better."[22] On another occasion, he pooh-poohed critics of suburban sprawl as, predictably, *snobs* who complained about traffic congestion and ugly shopping malls and who pined for outdated planning techniques that placed government at the center of things. These critics just could not accept the fact that "much of the planning" in America's new suburbs "is done by real estate developers," seemingly the true paragons of democracy for Barnes.[23] Following suit, television commentator and nationally syndicated columnist Charles Krauthammer could write a piece that characterized critics of the commercialization of professional sports as naysaying "purists."[24] And Michael Anton could celebrate the "hyper-entertaining of America," including the placement of televisions and radios in more public spaces and the recent "Disneyfication of Times Square." The cause of popular culture's omnipresence? "People really just like never-ending audio-visual stimulation, and why not?" This was, after all, the "first truly popular culture in human history."[25] Corporate capitalism gave the virtuous people what they wanted and deserved.

In this area of cultural and political cheerleading, there was one voice that dominated: David Brooks. Though he did not come from such honorable lineage as Podhoretz or Kristol, he was a leading figure in making conservatism more intellectually respectable and hip. One of his first (and lesser-known) projects was *Backward and Upward*, a collected set of essays that he edited the same year the *Weekly Standard* was founded. In his introduction to the book, Brooks told a story about struggling with a *New York Times Magazine* photographer who wanted to shoot his photo with his arms crossed and standing in a dark hallway. Brooks wanted to look more relaxed. The image mattered to Brooks, because he did not want to project an image of conservatives as "heavies." Brooks believed conservatives need not be brooding; they could be lighthearted and fun. His pose won him admiration, his sunnier personality allowing him to go where few conservative publicists had gone before—into the arms of the liberal media as an editorialist at the *New York Times* and as a commentator on PBS.[26]

Brooks consciously left behind the crusty social criticism associated with older conservatives such as Russell Kirk. Following Norman Podhoretz, he insisted intellectuals were just as materialistic and conformist as the masses.[27] He touted the elder Podhoretz's books *Making It* and *My Love Affair with America* and their autobiographical destruction of intellectual pomp.[28] Echoing Podhoretz's blast against the "adversary culture" and the "new class," Brooks castigated contemporary "bourgeoisophobes" who sneered at America's cult of success.[29]

Like Podhoretz's son, he wrote with an air of hip coolness as he mimicked the academic Left by turning consumerism into a form of democratic empowerment.

Indeed, for Brooks, consumerism is the quintessential expression of American greatness. With an abundance of goods available to all, power and hierarchy in society disappear. "Professors at Harvard think the corporate elites run society, while the corporate elites think the cultural elites at Harvard run society," Brooks quips, leaving the reader incapable of figuring out where power really resides but certain that it is not in the hands of a corporate elite (that's for elitist liberal snobs to believe). The bottom line suggests there is no power; corporate leaders hold no more influence than anyone else. Corporate marketeers simply follow the lead of ordinary citizens by providing an abundance of consumer goods that allows all to define themselves however they please. In the past, the wealthy might have exerted control and cultural hegemony (as Thorstein Veblen argued in his famous analysis of "conspicuous consumption"), but that is no longer the case. "Perhaps there was once such a pecking order, with the Vanderbilts and Rockefellers on top," Brooks argues. But "in the information age," he explains, "classes define themselves by their means of consumption." Consumption does not express power; all people—no matter what their standing in life—are free to change their clothes and lifestyle to express their true feelings. "There is no single elite in America," Brooks explains. "Everyone can be an aristocrat within his own Olympus." Or in other words, "Everything that was once hierarchical turns cellular."[30]

Brooks makes America appear a near-utopian democracy. But sometimes doubt seems to enter his writing. At times, he even sounds as if he is offering a devastating critique of suburban life. Take his dissection of "ubermoms" (Brooks follows Tom Wolfe's pop sociological tendency to create catchy classifications). Brooks explains that you can "spot" ubermoms "easily" at "board and parent-association meetings" because "they generally weigh less than their children." They might have "given birth to their youngest one, say, twelve hours before, but they still have washboard abs and buttocks firmer than footballs." At the time of conceiving her child, Brooks speculates, an ubermom is probably "staring at the ceiling calculating which year her child will be ready to enter nursery school" and preparing for her child's future of "school accountability tests, SAT exams, workplace aptitude measures" and making the requisite purchase of "Mozart for Babies CDs" that can "enhance the little one's early-life brain functions."[31]

Brooks has funny things to say about suburban males as well. For instance, he plows through recent issues of *Cigar Aficionado* magazine. Inviting its readers to submit photographs about their subculture's smoking habits, the magazine tenders often hilarious revelations. Brooks discusses what he thinks is the "best shot" he "ever saw." It "featured a cigar smoker crouching in front of his Corvette, with his three-car garage and two rider mowers visible in the background—a masterpiece of compressing all of one's penis-augmentation devices into one small photograph." This seems more like the Frankfurt School of yesterday than the hip cultural studies teachings of the academic Left, that is, more the language of cultural manipulation than empowerment.[32]

But in the end, ubermoms and cigar dads actually represent American greatness. Those who feel compelled to consume larger quantities of consumer goods and who gaze at the advertisements abundant everywhere are simply getting "pleasure from bathing in the possibility of what might be, of sloshing about in the golden waters of some future happiness." They are giving expression to their "longing to realize blissful tomorrows." They are not finding their desires channeled by mindless imitation, by social or corporate pressures, as they dream of purchasing a SUV. They are quite simply dreaming, thinking expansively about great things. They do not find their horizons and possibilities limited by the gridlock of the highway or the imperative to own at least one car to survive in the exurbs where the highways have to add a tenth lane; they just dream and drive on. Brooks's world is so open as to seem that there are no material forces that might actually limit peoples' horizons or dreams.[33]

It is odd to hear Brooks squeeze the greatness out of uber-moms and cigar dads. Consider *Cigar Aficionado* magazine again. Brooks says that many of the photographs found within "seem to confirm the stereotype of modern Americans as crass vulgarians." This tone quickly changes to a self-tortured writing style: "But if you study the impulse behind these shots with a kinder eye—which admittedly takes Ghandian forbearance—you do see the quintessential American impulse: to depict some perfect world in which money, friendship, comfort, pleasure, and success all roll into one to create perfect bliss." All is fine, even as we look at pictures of "sixty year old men" hanging out with "cosmetically enhanced women who wear gold lame E-Z Off party dresses." Nothing ugly or troubling, just good old American dreaming. "America is the solution to bourgeois flatness," Brooks explains, and you can almost hear him pinching out his words or looking over his shoulder, praying for no follow-up question. America is the "solution" to "mass-media shallowness," Brooks goes on climactically, "because America, with all its utopian possibilities, arouses the energies and the most strenuous efforts." Brooks's cultural populism turns swiftly into a celebration of America as a utopian democracy of heroic initiative.[34]

This self-satisfied paean to American greatness suggests a certain comfort creeping into the mini-con mind during the first years of the twenty-first century. With the victory of Bush in 2000, Brooks's celebration of America started to take a more distinctly populist direction. Conservatives already had a congressional majority when the *Weekly Standard* started in 1995. After it had been in existence for a year, Norman Podhoretz was asked to compare his son's magazine to *Commentary* in the 1970s. "We were a fairly lonely voice in opposition," he explained, "and that creates a different tone, and a different imperative for an editor, than when you've won, or are winning."[35] Five years after its founding, the *Weekly Standard* not only had Republicans in the congressional majority but the presidency. And then the horror of 9/11 hit, and Bush pushed for war in Iraq. Suddenly, the *Weekly Standard* became not just a hotbed for conservative cultural studies but also for vehement arguments on behalf of a growing Republican majority it believed was forming, as well as for Bush's foreign policy and, just as important, for the president's persona.[36]

Having articulated American greatness emanating from the new suburbs and the prosperity of the 1990s, the magazine's editors started to imagine American greatness projected outward long before 9/11 struck. Bill Kristol took the lead here, having helped form the Project for a New American Century in 1997, an organization that called for unilateral action on the part of the United States, including against Saddam Hussein. Kristol hoped to remake Iraq and spread democracy through the Middle East. And it is here that the utopian idealism of the 1960s clearly passed hands from left to right. In January 2002, Kristol was calling for extending the war against Afghanistan to Iraq—linking Hussein to the terrorists.[37] As the war became reality, Kristol cheered it on. He would write in 2003: "Duly armed, the United States can act to secure its safety and to advance the cause of liberty—in Baghdad and beyond."[38] The Vietnam legacy—the doubt about America's ability to do good abroad that Norman Podhoretz had already criticized—seemed finally vanquished. Even more than just vanquished—completely flushed out of the conservative mind. Kristol had turned Whittaker Chambers's and James Burnham's aggressive critique of containment during the Cold War into a call for unilateral action to remake the world along American ideals. This was rollback on steroids—fit for a new world order. And Kristol's message became downright utopian in its hope of remaking the world.

But the cause was not just Iraq, it was Bush himself. For here the postwar conservative mind found a totem for the themes that started coming together at the time—utopianism, distrust in intellectuals, and populism. Fred Barnes made it clear what he and other conservative intellectuals liked about Bush's style—the president's utopian dreams about the world bending to America's hopes and his penchant as a rebel fighting the naysayers. For Barnes, Bush was a "defiant" rebel ready to battle a society of conformists, a radical and utopian whose spirit went directly back to the 1960s. And, as Podhoretz the younger put it, President Bush had pioneered this style of rebellion all the while driving "liberals insane," updating Goldwater's cowboy swagger. The conservative as brash rebel remaking the world—it was a perfect remaking of 1960s style, and it was found in the standing president. Bush served as a symbol for broadest principles of the conservative mind.[39]

Of course, the optimism of 2003–2004 started to slip. In May 2003, the *Weekly Standard* declared "VICTORY" in bold letters on its cover, alongside a picture of Bush standing on the now infamous USS *Abraham Lincoln* with that now infamous banner reading "Mission Accomplished" unfurled behind him. In 2004, mini-con Podhoretz the younger was arguing that the wars in Afghanistan and Iraq would "serve as the blueprint for martial conflict for the foreseeable future."[40] Just a year later, this sort of triumphalism was dashed. The war took a turn for the worse, and the *Weekly Standard* editors' close association with Bush caused chafing. Utopian claims made in 2003 sounded absurd just three years later. *Weekly Standard* editors started calling for stability (necessitating more troops) rather than liberty and democracy, and the utopian project of conservative intellectuals seemed to lie like wreckage in the sands of Iraq. [41] One hope remained: Iraq was not necessarily the most important war the conservative mind was fighting at the time.

APOCALYPSE NOW: THE CULTURE WARS
AS NEW DEFINING MOMENT

The postwar conservative mind was born into a state of battle and apocalypse, trying to charge up Americans' view of the Cold War with their fervent ideals. This mindset of catastrophe—formed during a foundational moment—never exited the conservative mind. And throughout the 1990s, a new set of culture wars—fought at home—became all the more important in structuring the thinking of conservatives. By the 1970s, culture wars were already bubbling up in America. Televangelists like Jerry Falwell called for the renewal of traditional morality against "secular humanism." Debates surrounding abortion and sex education erupted during the 1970s, and by the 1990s these debates conjoined with those surrounding gay marriage.

In three major conservative battles that emerged during the 1990s and moved into the 2000s—the legislative push to police America's colleges to cut down on "liberal bias," the introduction of "intelligent design" in public schools, and the continuing war against the "liberal media"—postmodern conservatism crystallized in more perfect form than in debates surrounding Iraq. Crossing the postmodern divide, conservatives came out the other side stronger. The conservative mind drew on the battles lines fixed earlier by the New Right over public school textbooks and abortion and ingested them into its own permanent psychic state. David Horowitz would call these "wars of aggression"; Coulter would speak of "throttling" liberals. Out of the struggles of war the postmodern conservative mind emerged more clearly.

Regulating the Academy

Ever since William Buckley wrote *God and Man at Yale*, academia had focused the ire of the conservative mind. Gaining political power during the 1990s, conservatives grew annoyed that their reach did not extend to the university. New leftists ("tenured radicals") still seemed to hold all the power there. For conservative writers, academia was now a hotbed of multiculturalism, speech codes, political correctness, identity politics, and an incoherent canon that had thrown out the "great books" tradition of yore. And academe for conservative intellectuals throughout the 1990s symbolized liberalism writ large. Conservatives pummeled the postmodern university, blaming liberalism for shoddy education (Alan Bloom's *The Closing of the American Mind* [1987] and Dinesh D'Souza's *Illiberal Education* [1991] key among them), but these books did not change anything. The problem demanded bolder activism—something more akin to war.

Enter once again the gladiator David Horowitz armed with his "second thoughts." In 2003, he helped form Students for Academic Freedom (SAF). Some might have thought the organization modeled itself on the Young Americans for Freedom (YAF), student activists on the Right who upheld loyalty oaths for professors during the Cold War. But instead SAF mimicked the academic Left. "I encourage" students, Horowitz explained, "to use the language that the left has deployed so effectively on behalf of its own agendas. Radical professors have created a 'hostile learning' environment for conservative students. . . . The university should be an 'inclusive' and intellectually 'diverse' community."[42] Horowitz clicked off the key words of the academic Left to justify right-wing student activism. To embolden the cause of right-wing "diversity," Horowitz drafted the "student bill of rights," which is now referred to as the Academic Bill of Rights (ABOR), a boilerplate piece of legislation that scolded liberal professors for indoctrinating their students and encouraged state legislatures to police higher education classrooms to ensure intellectual diversity. Starting in 2004, Horowitz pushed for its passage in numerous states.[43]

Horowitz took up the tradition of conservative activism against academe and went in new directions. Buckley's rebel stance hovered like a friendly ghost around Horowitz's activism. After all, pissing off tenured radicals seemed one of Horowitz's greatest ambitions (see his *The Professors: 101 Most Dangerous Academics in America*). But Buckley had been an absolutist on questions surrounding academic freedom, and Horowitz had turned postmodern. Buckley wrote: "It is my view that as long as academic freedom takes the implied position that all ideas are equal, or that all ideas should, in the student's mind, start out equal, it is a dangerous . . . concept."[44] Horowitz reversed this logic, his idea of intellectual "diversity" growing out of contemporary theories about the indeterminacy of knowledge. Here is the original ABOR statement: "Human knowledge is a never-ending pursuit of the truth" because "there is no humanly accessible truth that is not in principle open to challenge, and . . . no party or intellectual faction has a monopoly on wisdom."[45] Though Horowitz shared Buckley's vision, he also knew that the terms of activism and intellectual politics had changed.

Horowitz also knew that he could play on popular strains of anti-intellectualism and populist hatred of academe. He directly inherited the neoconservative attack against the "new class" and the New Right's tirades against "pointy-headed" intellectuals. But he went one step further by arguing for legislation that would allow state legislatures to police classrooms because professors would not police their own members. Professional codes of conduct simply shrouded power and domination. The professoriate would never stop imposing its political views on college students unless policed by the state. ABOR called for the "protection of students" from "the imposition of any orthodoxy of a political, religious or ideological nature."[46] Horowitz combined this paternalistic language with the political language of the 1960s. He pierced claims to objectivity, arguing that professors simply wanted to indoctrinate young minds with liberal ideology.[47] Horowitz echoed the writers at the *Intercollegiate Review* who questioned scientific neutrality and professional objectivity, but he hardened the critique. He also sounded like Michel Foucault delineating an inherent nexus between knowledge and

power, discovering the conservative benefits of postmodern
theory.

Horowitz's activism conjures memories of New Left radicalism in other ways. Right-wing students demanding the curriculum reflect their own ideological orientation sound a lot like
students who wanted "relevant" curriculum during the 1960s
that would help them understand Vietnam. The language of
"rights" and participatory democracy also live on in Horowitz's
activism, conceptualizing, as it does, the student as a consumer of
academic goods and thus sharing a voice in their delivery (again,
an echo of Buckley could be heard). Both right-wing students and
their New Left progenitors exerted pressure that challenges
claims to institutional stability and professional authority. After
all, Horowitz encouraged right-wing students to police classrooms and document bias. One offshoot from ABOR is a bill in
Arizona that would force professors to provide "alternative
coursework" if students "find the assigned material 'personally
offensive.' "[48] The utter absurdity of such a program seems obvious, loading up institutions with ridiculous demands. Though
Horowitz disagrees with this particular version of legislation, it
clearly sprang from his own ABOR activity, and it is hard to see
how it diverges from his own thought. It simply pushes the
demand that students determine their own education to its logical conclusion and flows from a belief in empowering students
and the language of consumerism.

Horowitz also assumes that winning political power ensures
cultural transformation. After two years of SAF activism, Horowitz
reflected on the 2004 presidential election and stated: "The election is a big boost for the academic bill of rights, no question."[49]
One of the sponsors he linked up with in late 2004 made the
connection between political power and the right to police
classrooms explicit, illustrating the dangerous blowback for an
intellectual-activist alliance on the Right. Larry Mumper, a state
senator from Ohio, endorsed ABOR and asked: "Why should we

as fairly moderate to conservative legislators continue to support universities that turn out students who rail against the very policies that their parents voted us in for?"[50] Buckley's desire for the executive power of alumni and trustees acting through the university president was now placed in the hands of state legislatures. Any remnant of Buckley's elitism is thrown out for a closer approximation of Willmoore Kendall's democratic majoritarianism. Horowitz champions populist democracy amassing power in the halls of state legislatures and then transforming the university.

Horowitz's activism on behalf of right-wing students exemplifies the postmodern conservative mindset. He sees knowledge as relative and celebrates diversity and plurality. He believes politics is king and that power always colors any claim to objectivity. And he sees his activism as a legitimate and rightful inheritance of the 1960s spirit. Tenured radicals with poststructuralist ideas bouncing around in their minds might be the embodiment of the 1960s to some, but so too is Horowitz. Call it the horseshoe effect of cultural politics in the age of postmodernity—the academic Left and postmodern Right coming full circle. Horowitz's own biographical zigzags suggest that this should not come as a surprise.

Intelligent Design

If conservatives have traditionally questioned academia for its liberal machinations, their dislike of modern science has become no less pronounced. Go back to the Cold War and listen to the conservative intellectual Frank Meyer complaining about liberalism's "science-worship."[51] Conservatives nurtured their own romantic streak, one that perceived limits to materialism and scientific inquiry. Whittaker Chambers—who excommunicated Rand in part for what today would be called her "logocentrism"—believed science had displaced marveling at the "wonder of life and the wonder of the universe, the wonder of life within the wonder of the universe." As he sat at the breakfast table and examined his daughter's ear with its beautiful features, Chambers came to believe that "design presupposes God," that nature could not be explained by coldhearted scientific rationalism.[52]

Whereas Buckley's rebel stance informed the late 1950s and 1960s, Chambers's critique of science found odd inheritors during the 1960s. The critique found resonance in America's counterculture. As the leading theorist of the counterculture, Theodore Roszak pointed out in 1969: "The leading mentors of our youthful counterculture have . . . called into question the validity of the conventional scientific world view" (this included Herbert Marcuse's critique of technological rationality). The young, Roszak believed, were "dropping out" of a technocratic system built on the prosperity ensured by science and technology. When hippies "returned to nature" and kids started drifting away from Christianity toward Eastern mysticism (Shamanism and Zen), they were embracing a "magical world view" that renewed the sort of wonder about the world Chambers had experienced with his daughter's ear at the breakfast table. The "scientific world view" no longer persuaded the young. Science's authority collapsed, much like the authority of parents and government.[53]

The counterculture's impact and shockwaves were felt long after the 1960s, though the more radical and transformative talk of Roszak became quickly dated, blowing away like so much marijuana smoke. Still, academic postmodernists who worked in philosophy and history continued to argue that science's foundations were more historically rooted and less objective than previously believed. The writings of philosophers of science like Thomas Kuhn and Paul Feyarbend most explicitly explored these themes, and their criticisms resonated with the academic Left and its theories about the indeterminacy of knowledge developed in philosophy and English departments. Generally though, doubts about science drifted back to the right—especially as the New Right pressed an evangelical basis for conservative activism. Conservative intellectuals criticized scientists' amoral outlook about genetic engineering and their tendency to see biological roots to all behavior, as they questioned the immorality of abortion. They famously attacked Terri Schiavo's husband for pulling the feeding tube that sustained her life—analogizing his action to abortion, the taking of life. But it was the call to teach "intelligent design" in public schools that became the most important movement critical of science and constitutive of postmodern conservatism. Here, conservative intellectuals did not just criticize science's power; they offered a new vision to explain the world.[54]

"Intelligent design" (ID) is typically understood as an updated version of biblical creationism, a view that seemed to have disappeared from public sight after the Scopes trial of 1925. But "intelligent design" offered something creationism had not. It did not begin with the biblical story of creation but rather with doubts about Darwin's explanations of evolution, a distinctly postmodern starting point. In 1996, ID's leading exponents formed a think tank called the Discovery Institute, based in Seattle. Led by Phillip Johnson, the author of *Darwin on Trial* (1991), a leading evangelical critic of evolution, and a demi-intellectual of sorts, the writers and publicists gathered here came up with the "teach the controversy" approach to presenting ID, sometimes called the "wedge" strategy (named after a controversial paper of uncertain authorship known as the "Wedge Document" that appeared on the Internet in 1999 and showed how antievolution activism could help "replace materialistic explanations with the theistic understanding that nature and human beings are created by God").[55] The Discovery Institute has offered fellowships to writers and support for grassroots initiatives (that created numerous successes) in states like Ohio, Kansas, and Texas, and they have argued that Darwinian evolution is one theory that should be taught alongside other

theories, including Chamber's argument that "design presupposes God."[56]

ID proponents argue that teachers have the right and responsibility to expose students to diverse viewpoints about evolution. In 2001, Senator Rick Santorum used that rationale to
introduce a Senate amendment promoting ID and tied it to the
No Child Left Behind Act (this ultimately failed), and President
Bush echoed it a few years later in 2005 when he lent his support
to the movement.[57] "Both sides ought to be properly taught so
people can understand what the debate is about," the president
explained, implying that liberal teachers were repressing diversity in America's classrooms. The goal of introducing ID into the
classroom was to "expose people to different schools of thought."[58]
Exponents of ID have, in the words of the *New York Times*, successfully "transformed the debate into an issue of academic freedom rather than a confrontation between biology and religion."[59]
As Horowitz mined the postmodern concept that all knowledge
is indeterminate in order to justify ABOR, defenders of ID
embrace the postmodern view of science as one of many "paradigms" that help human beings make sense of their world.

The history of this movement is more detailed than my
treatment here suggests (indeed, an entire book about the movement was published in 2004). And there are numerous less-
well-known intellectuals arguing its case. But most important in
this context is the *style* of argument made on ID's behalf. No scientists confirm the nature of the arguments made by ID'ers, which
allows figures like Phillip Johnson to think of themselves as
rebels against a steadfast liberal establishment. Because of this,
postmodern theories have informed their battle plans. "Teach
the controversy" is indebted, after all, to the postmodern doubts
about truth being singular. Johnson once explained: "I'm
no postmodernist," but "I've learned a lot" from reading postmodern theory. This makes his thinking, as he put it, "dead-bang
mainstream" in "academia these days."[60] In this, he is certainly

right. Like Horowitz, Johnson has taken up the language of radical relativism and postmodern theories of knowledge in order to do battle against the "liberal establishment"—all for the purpose of conservative aims and giving insight into a mindset framed by the necessity of war.

Undermining the "Liberal Media"

Those who have studied the success of ID admire its well-orchestrated media and publicity campaign. Most proponents of the theory are not working in laboratories garnering counter-evidence to Darwin's findings. They are, instead, writing for a wider public and mobilizing action at the state and local level. The success of the movement is the result of the conservative movement's capacity to transform the world of the mass media and to a decline in citizens' view of journalistic ethics over the past few years. And this brings us to the final culture war that informs the contemporary conservative mind.

This book has already shown how conservatives battled the "liberal media" throughout postwar American history. Complaints about the media littered the pages of the *National Review* during the 1950s, and Barry Goldwater's run prompted more. In 1964, M. Stanton Evans argued that "managed news" shut Barry Goldwater out of the mainstream.[61] This view found more prominent voices during the late 1960s. In 1969, Vice President Spiro Agnew famously berated television news as hostile to President Richard Nixon's oversight of the Vietnam War. He condemned television news shows' "instant analysis and querulous criticism" perpetrated by a "small band of network commentators and self-appointed analysts, the majority of whom" were hostile to Nixon. Television news people were "urbane" and lived within "the geographical and intellectual confines of Washington D.C., or New York City." Agnew took Evans's critique and pushed it in more explicitly populist directions, a touch of Kevin Phillips's Wallace-ism added to the mix.[62]

Two years later, Edith Efron, a right-wing writer at *TV Guide*, would blast liberal "bias" in her best-selling book *The News Twisters* (1971). The book was chock full of charts showing that, indeed, Spiro Agnew was right: the press *had* treated Nixon harshly. From there, Efron argued that the FCC fairness doctrine and the First Amendment were too broadly interpreted. "The First Amendment," she wrote, "gives the press the right to be biased." For instance, it allowed the mainstream media to treat the "white middle class" and "provincial" people with disdain. The media also flattered the New Left, or what she referred to as "the kids." She believed a "silent majority" would rise up in revolt against the press's bias (her argument won an invitation to Nixon's White House that she declined). And then in passing, Efron pointed out something else: that "study after study has revealed that people buy publications with whose editorials they agree." This insight, more than her call for a revolt on the part of the silent majority, transformed the future of the mass media.[63]

Efron's view worked in tandem with the initiatives of "new journalists" who were writing around the same time and had questioned the importance of "objectivity" in reporting. During the late 1960s, the new sensibility joined the world of journalism—witnessed in the pioneering work of Tom Wolfe and Joan Didion (the latter had written for *National Review* briefly). It reached its fruition in the work of Podhoretz's hero Norman Mailer, especially his *Armies of the Night* (a book he cleverly described, following Truman Capote, as a historical novel) that described his own interaction with New Left protesters against the Vietnam War. The book was, in typical Mailer fashion, as much about Mailer as it was the event described—a major protest against the Pentagon. Hunter S. Thompson wrote in a similar vein by documenting his own hallucinatory escapades in *Fear and Loathing in Las Vegas* and then his own reactions to the 1972 political conventions in his *Fear and Loathing on the Campaign Trail*. New journalism's *subjectivity*—its faith that the

reporter's consciousness deserved attention—was easily radicalized into profound doubt about the possibility of *any* objective
treatment of events. This was the postmodern kernel in the
movement. New journalism could be understood as a product of
the 1960s, but it could also be gleaned in the *National Review*'s
early editorial in favor of a "personal journalism—the manly
presentation of deeply felt convictions" and necessarily an
accompanying ethic of "controversy." That did not sound all that
different from Tom Wolfe's original definition of new journalism
as "personality, energy, drive, bravura."[64]

Efron's argument that consumers buy the media they prefer
and the rebellion against objectivity found in the work of new
journalists helped clear the way for the "new" media that defines
our own age: cable television with its widespread choice and a
plurality of "political" news shows; the Internet with its "search-
driven culture" and opinionated blogs; and talk radio, a medium
highly favorable to populist rantings with explicit partisan leanings. All of these outlets have effectively dismantled the ideal of
"objective" journalism, as do the incessant complaints about the
mainstream media—now labeled simply MSM—by conservative
writers and their search for a more authentic "personal journalism."

Just how far these changes have gone and how much the
Right is responsible for them can be seen in the stodgier world
of book publishing. Today, niche marketing has generated an
array of conservative book publishers (or divisions within existing
houses): Random House's Crown forum, Penguin's imprint
Sentinel, Simon and Schuster's Threshold Editions (run by Mary
Matalin), Encounter Books in San Francisco, and the oldest conservative publisher, Regnery. Publishers hunt for opinionated
and bold arguments that can be marketed to well-defined political audiences. Judith Regan, once an editor at Pocket Books
(Simon and Schuster) who signed Sean Hannity (and more
memorably O. J. Simpson), explained: "What people respond
to in this culture is loud and brash and pointed and sometimes

vulgar—that's what gets people's attention, on TV and radio
and in books. Shades-of-gray books are very difficult to sell."[65]
Publishers now promote conservative books that are clearly
tagged as such—books by Coulter, Savage, O'Reilly—through a
well-defined segment of networks, including conservative Web
sites and magazines, Fox News, right-wing talk radio, and right-
wing book clubs. Shock and sensationalism help sell conservative books, even if such values seem in conflict with conservative
values.

By the mid-1990s, some conservatives were honest enough
to admit that they had transformed the MSM.[66] In essence, the
"counterestablishment" of the *National Review* and a few other
publications now started to look more like a full-fledged postmodern establishment, if such a term makes sense. In 1996, one
writer for the *Weekly Standard* explained that conservatives dominated talk radio and some television outlets, "from Limbaugh to
the Capital Gang." Talk radio, of course, was a medium that
reached large numbers with no pretense of professionalism or
objectivity, and it carried with it a more widespread revolution
in the media. This same *Weekly Standard* author went on to explain
that the liberal media—with its air of "press-as-clerisy"—would
reject the "new regime of radio gas-bags, TV shoutathons, and
Internet yahoos."[67] But the revolution *would* be televised and
could not be held back by the elite trying to suppress the populist rage that Efron could only dream about. This new conservative counterregime would soon include Fox News and then
Internet "blogs."[68] Conservatives created a new media landscape
that blurred the line between news and opinion, eliciting a profoundly postmodern cultural victory. As Nicholas Lemann
pointed out: "Conservatives are relativists when it comes to the
press. In their view, nothing is neutral: there is no disinterested
version of the news; everything reflects politics and relationships
to power and cultural perspective."[69] That was the essence of their
revolt and its transformational success in making a new world

fraught with cultural fragmentation and dissonance—today's world of postmodernity.

THE ENDGAME OF POSTMODERN CONSERVATISM

The postmodernism of MSM critics, ID proponents, and ABOR activists work in tandem. So too does the celebration of popular culture by hipster conservatives at the *Weekly Standard* and the rantings of Coulter and Savage that further segment readers. Other critics have noticed a growing postmodern streak in conservative activism and thought today. For instance, the literary critic Stanley Fish believes ID proponents adopt postmodern ideas for the sake of strategy, to win influence and to wedge their ideas into a culture that rejects absolutist claims. But in reality the strategy is much more pervasive than Fish's interpretation suggests; postmodernity frames numerous culture wars fought by the postwar conservative mind and has helped create something resembling a ragtag establishment—an establishment that glorifies rebellion, loudmouthed rantings, a debunking of professional authority, and a relativist view of truth. Postmodern conservatism has been much more transformational than the term "strategy" suggests.

What critics like Stanley Fish miss (most likely because they want to hold on to their own left-leaning postmodernism) is that the conservative mind was a mind born in a state of war and the rebel style was one of its key weapons. Its sense of apocalypse and righteousness lends itself to the use of whatever means necessary—including relativistic tactics. It is not that the conservative mind adopts relativism and postmodernism as tools that are simply strategic in nature, slyly chosen to make headway. It is that the mindset of war propels fervent choices of warlike tactics. These are not just convenient tools being adapted, they are weapons—weapons that reflect the apocalyptic mindset making the choice. The tactics and the mindset are much more closely wedded than critics like Fish imagine. And the tactics and mind-set make for the odd combination of fervent absolutism matched with postmodern relativism.

Postmodern conservatism grows out of the cultural radicalism of the 1960s, and it is the logical conclusion of a conservative mind born in rebellion during the 1950s that embraced an apocalyptic sense of the Cold War. Conservatives have rarely conserved or stood in defense of the status quo; instead, they have rebelled against America's status quo—against a "liberal establishment" they demand be torn down and that now seems fairly-well defeated. From Buckley's era onward, conservative intellectuals stoked anger and raw energy, and contemporary pundits like Ann Coulter have simply pushed that project to its logical extreme. The confrontational and apocalyptic spirit of the 1960s resonates in the conservative mind of today. From William Buckley's rebel yell against the Yale administration to the attack on the "new class" by the neoconservatives to the populist wrath against pointy-headed intellectuals by the New Right to David Horowitz's Academic Bill of Rights, conservative intellectuals have always embraced a radical democratic streak, populist tones, and anti-intellectualism, all of which culminate today.

Conservatives have consistently dreamed of something more than just political victory. They have desired cultural transformation, and they now have the right to claim some success. The "liberal establishment" is in tatters. The term "liberalism" itself is rarely uttered, let alone defended, in public. Replacing the liberal establishment is a new postmodern culture framed in large part by conservative arguments and ideas and helped out ironically by numerous arguments found on the academic Left. For instance, we have come to think of political discussion as most entertaining when it takes the form of shouting—the way Buckley went for rebellious shock in his critique of Yale and Horowitz speaks of a contemporary "war of aggression." When Ann Coulter talks of boiling liberals in oil or driving opponents into a rage, she is playing the role of the conservative thinker inherited from William Buckley and juicing it up to fit a culture that prizes explosive rants more than reasoned debate. Today, shouting to one's predestined audience matters more than reaching the wider public. Civility be damned. Why worry when power is on your side or will be?

As postmodern conservative intellectuals have waged their wars, they have helped create a culture in which the fine art of discerning truth from falsehood seems unnecessary. A culture in which the line between news and opinion no longer holds, where all truth-claims are shields covering up political belief and prejudice. A culture that is disrespectful of professional competence and holds intelligence in contempt, pilloried as elitism and snobbery. A culture that no longer thinks it important to discern high from low or good argument from bad so long as entertainment is found. The examples of extremism that I noted at the beginning of this book are part and parcel of the conservative mind as it has grown more confident throughout the postwar years and more willing to embrace the anti-intellectual and populist style of American political culture. Talk of pompous intellectuals by Russell Kirk and the political and moral talk of the "new class" during the 1970s by neoconservatives and New Right intellectuals alike—this is the foundation on which the conservative mind has built. The extremism is the endgame—the logical conclusion of a mind at war with a fledgling enemy.

The utopianism of the conservative mind—its faith in its own capacity to remake the world—has certainly faltered in the deserts of Iraq. The hubris has been evident as citizens watch a war first described as a "cakewalk" with instantaneous "Mission Accomplished" turn into a long, drawn-out mess. And so the conservative mind's postmodern utopianism necessarily rejects the countervailing power of reality, embodied in the statement made by a Bush administration aide to the journalist Ron Suskind at the height of the Iraq War: "We're an empire now, and when we act, we create our own reality. And while you're studying that reality—judiciously as you will—we'll act again, creating other new realities, which you can study."[70] *Making* reality—that says it all about postmodern conservatism today. The foibles of Iraq are the generalized foibles of the conservative mind. And the results are clear.

But there is no reason to believe that any of this will stop the conservative mind, activism, or style from hurtling forward. David Horowitz has too much gleam in his eyes to stop anytime soon. Ann Coulter seems too angry and seems to do too well in book sales to wonder if there is something corrosive about yelling at and demonizing opponents. ID proponents have won too many victories to wonder if perhaps their own relativistic conception of knowledge might do damage to education or respect for scientific inquiry. And the *Weekly Standard* editors are just too hip to wonder if popular culture and suburban sprawl might not be the utopian agents they want them to be. The post-war conservative mind has unleashed new forces that feed into the populist and anti-intellectual tendencies deeply rooted in American history, and this has won it popularity. Today, it becomes imperative for critics of the conservative mind to point out how it threatens our fragile civil culture, our faith in professions and scientific knowledge, our ability to discern facts from political opinion, and the general pursuit of the life of the mind. In the end, "wars of aggression" create blowback and damage. We should not forget that.

CONCLUSION

When Extremism Becomes a Virtue

IMAGINE FOR A MOMENT A SCAFFOLDING. That is the image of the postwar conservative mind drawn here. It possesses coherency, but a polyglot coherency carved from different moments in the past. To note this is not new. George Nash, in his classic work about conservative intellectuals originally published thirty years ago, explained that the conservative mind was "a compound of diverse and not always consistent impulses." Other observers have pointed out the conservative tension between a faith in free markets (individualism) and traditional social order (communitarianism) or between a belief in energetic foreign policy (rollback and the Bush Doctrine) and small government. But I have added to these a less noted tension between absolutist principles and a relativistic outlook on tactics. Call it the mind of apocalyptic war as a permanent feature of the conservative mind.[1]

Holding contradictory positions at the same time does not necessarily entail crisis or weakness; it can, in fact, create strength. The merger of absolutism and postmodern relativism, for instance, might appear schizophrenic, prone to shakiness or explosion. But in reality, the mindset of apocalyptic war and embrace of relativistic means work well together. Believing in war—including its destructive nature—for the sake of absolutist principles is no contradiction. The conservative mind is a "mind on fire," to use Emerson's evocative phrase. For sure, sometimes the conservative mind threatens to burn itself out, to ignite, explode, and smolder away. But the mind's burning has usually welded disparate elements together into a white-hot unity.

Some readers might detect a dialectical interpretation of the conservative mind in this book. Though I reject teleology, my story provides something like a thesis, antithesis, and synthesis. There's the original Old Right style of rebellion (Buckley and his allies) and populism counterpoised by the neoconservative antithesis (with its critique of populism) and then the final synthesis of postmodern conservatism. In the end, the Old Right—as a dialectical read would suggest—shares with the postmodern conservatism more than some might think—precisely because of the internal logic of the conservative mind's motor (shown in my opening comparison between Buckley and Coutler's shared style). Throughout history, the conservative mind generates internal criticisms: first, Peter Viereck's respectable conservatism (denounced by Frank Meyer) or Ayn Rand's rationalistic libertarianism (thrown overboard by Whittaker Chambers) and then the more centrist elements of neoconservative hand-wringing (transcended by New Right populists and postmodern, conservative hipsters). Criticisms are purged or engorged, and then the conservative mind grows stronger as a result.

In trying to paint a picture of a conflicted but ultimately unified mind, I have emphasized certain ideas over others. But I have also admitted diversity, not a simple unification. American conservatism could not be just one thing, because American political culture is not just one thing. Building a conservative mind with appeal required building a polyglot mind. Still, critics will complain that I have not focused on the single element they take as most important. For instance, some might wonder why I have not paid as much attention to libertarianism—a feature of the American conservative mind that has received a great deal of attention recently. The libertarian streak is certainly powerful. Nonetheless, as Whittaker Chambers's critique of Ayn Rand suggested, conservatism could never be entirely libertarian. It had to have a religious dimension—both in domestic and foreign policy terms—if it wanted to fit America's popular culture. The conservative had to be pluralist, never giving complete dominance to one element over another. And that pluralism demands more attention than each individual part.[2]

My emphasis on tension and movement, however, is not meant to ignore the overriding passion of the conservative mind: its rebellion against a once-strong and now defunct liberal establishment. The conservative has become a raucous hell-raiser tearing down structures. That is the style the conservative mind has embraced through the years. This explains key features of the mindset like populism, anti-intellectualism, and distrust in political authority or claims to professional competence, as well as why the 1960s served to the advantage of the conservative intellectual movement, both in positive and negative terms. Bush's persona—and the conservative intellectual celebration of it—is simply the latest manifestation of the conservative mind's internal workings, its love of tough-talking bravura, boldness, and aura of rebellion.

Let us mull over the term "rebel" for a moment, a word that possesses numerous meanings. For the time being, consider the image of rebellion in *The Wild One*, a classic film that codified the view of the tough-ass young hood that became so central to 1950s America and that correlates with the beginning of my story. Johnny, played by the ever-diffident Marlon Brando, heads up a motorcycle gang that comes into a small town and raises hell. Johnny's the perfect rebel: he hates cops and authority figures. There is also a narcissism to his defiance, an obsession about wanting to get the girl (in this case, the daughter of the local police chief) and wanting to project his micro-power. The rebel combines both elements—defiance and narcissism. After all, he is alienated and angry, and that alienation and anger constitute the rebel's actions in society. He consistently places his own

self-expression above the demands of social order. Or as Fred
Barnes described the conservative hero George W. Bush, the
rebel is "defiant," "scornful," and "blunt." The self's impatience
outweighs society's demands.[3]

My criticism might appear ironic, sounding like a conservative critique of conservatism. Perhaps, but it offers an explanation
of the stories told here, including Buckley's original takedown
of Yale during the 1950s, Evans's and Kirk's fascination with
campus rebels throughout the 1960s, Norman Podhoretz's "new
sensibility" and love of all things Mailer, and the strange resem-
blance between postmodern relativists and contemporary conservatives engaging in culture wars against the worlds of science,
the media, and academia. The rebel stance can also be discerned
in the contemporary conservative tendency to be rude, confrontational, and in-your-face. Ann Coulter and Michael Savage,
after all, are not sophisticates preserving social order; they are
rowdies who love the throttle of cultural battle. *Rebels all.*

This book tells a success story, but one with a cost. The conservative mind has triumphed as it learned to fit America's popular
culture, especially our culture's antiauthoritarianism and anti-
intellectualism. But the successes have bred problems as well.
The conservative mind is not all-powerful or impervious to
challenge. When Ann Coulter recently called John Edwards a
"faggot" for no explicable reason other than continuing her
penchant for rudeness and shock, her column was dropped from
numerous media outlets, and she was duly criticized by fellow
conservative pundits. The conservative "smashmouth" tendency
can wear thin. After all, Fox News's ratings are not what they
used to be.

Of course, the biggest failure of the conservative mind has
occurred in the deserts of Iraq. If ever there was a "war made
by intellectuals"—the term Randolph Bourne once used to describe liberal support for World War I—Iraq was it. The rebellious

utopianism of the conservative mind might just be careening to a skid in Iraq. The desire to remake the world in an ideal image—the motivation that animated the radical portions of the New Left during the 1960s and the motivation that underlay the optimistic visions of Bush's war in Iraq—that desire is now seen for what it was all along: a grandiose political vision doomed to failure. The tough stance of the rebel scowling at the world— "bring them on!" replacing "show me what you got"—has certainly grown a bit weaker in the knees. The rebel style might be conducive to standing outside the establishment and hurling invective but is not conducive to the fine art of governing. As critics like Alan Wolfe have already pointed out, the Bush administration succeeded at affirming its ideology and support from the "base," but it has not governed very well. The rebel stance is bold, and that helps explain its appeal. But the rebel stance also fails to generate authority, especially the sort that relies on accountability—something the rebel necessarily eschews.[4]

Though the conservative intellectual movement is not omnipotent, we must give credit where credit is due: it has succeeded at transforming our political culture. Just try to make an argument on behalf of objectivity or professionalism in journalism, and you will quickly find just how transformative the Right has been over the years. Or try to suggest that our culture should respect the world of academe. Or if you really want to try something wild, try to defend liberalism today. That's when you will really recognize the extent of the conservative mind's success over the years.

The success story is unlikely to end, for the conservative mind has found a permanent existence in its status as rebel. After all, the rebel always finds a reason to rebel. And the conservative mind has found that reason in liberalism, or more accurately, its own definition of liberalism throughout the years. In the 1950s, conservative intellectuals equated liberalism with communism and an establishment selling the country out to evil abroad.

Throughout the 1960s, conservatives argued that liberalism provided shelter and cover for the radical student Left. From that point on, conservatives projected onto liberalism their worst fears. By the 1990s, liberalism was feminism, animal rights, political correctness on college campuses, President Clinton's blow job (and the excuses made for it), weakness and sissiness, drinking lattes and hating rednecks, abortions, and elitism. Then with Bush's presidency, as writers at the *Weekly Standard* wrote in endless articles, liberalism became the zaniest of antiwar protesters, Michael Moore, or anyone who seemed in a perpetual state of anger at Bush's presidency.[5]

Conservatives vilified liberalism with panache. Their success has made liberalism one of the least-understood political philosophies in America today. As difficult as it is, it is time to say something about the conservative mind's enemy, to push back against the stereotyping of liberalism endemic to the conservative project. Of course, this is not the right place to provide a long disquisition on the merits of liberalism. But it seems appropriate to challenge some of the inaccuracies about liberalism that are at the cortex of the conservative mind and its arguments.

Unfortunately, some liberals hope to evade the conservative mind's culture wars altogether. Liberals have been so stereotyped on the battlefields of culture that many fear ever entering them again. Instead, many liberals today argue for "economic populism"—policies that support working people against corporate globalization, declining wages, and rising health-care costs—in order to circumvent the culture wars. Economic populism is certainly one part of liberalism, but *only* one part. Liberalism has a cultural vision that cannot be reduced to economic populism. Besides, populism, as I have pointed out throughout this book, carries too much problematic baggage. As a political theory, it degenerates into a mindless celebration of people as they are, without expecting anything from them in return—the people as a big mass backdrop on which to paint your own political arguments. That is why populism fires up the conservative mind: *Screw taxes because people hate them. Celebrate the Disneyfication of pop culture because everyone loves it. Lambaste the pointy-headed intellectuals because the people get jazzed up on that sort of thing.* Liberals today suggest fighting back with their own populist screams—redirecting them, of course, against the corporate elite rather than the government or intellectuals. But the limits of this counterpopulism seem immediately apparent. For instance, how does populism allow us to confront issues like global warming or science education in public schools or proposals to encourage legislatures to police classrooms against liberal indoctrination or the state of our media and professional integrity? The populist card can only be played so far.

Instead of evading the culture wars, liberals should explain the virtues necessary for a healthy polity—precisely those virtues the conservative mind negates. Consider this first principle: a liberal polity requires a democratic civic culture and public sphere built on trust and respect. For citizens to govern themselves—to learn the "liberal arts"—they must be educated and have the capacity to engage in rational discussions that move them beyond their preexisting passions and opinions. A good liberal citizen is one who listens and engages with a diverse set of views on a variety of issues and who pushes public discussion forward. The liberal citizen does not immediately shout at opponents or reach for charged rhetoric to win battles; there must be a sense of irony and self-questioning at the heart of a liberal citizen's public engagement. Therefore, liberalism's virtues include public-mindedness, rationality, humility, and autonomy. Faith in public deliberation requires citizens to hold to the ideal that there is some form of truth grounded in well-reasoned arguments rather than prejudice. Respecting the religious pluralism of modern life, liberalism encourages citizens to argue in terms understood by all, including secularists and members of different faiths. There must be a public language—grounded in rationality—that frames debate in a liberal society. None of the characteristics listed here as part of a liberal vision should sound all that new; numerous political theorists have explained "liberal virtues" elsewhere. I cannot do them justice here but only argue they exist, against what the conservative mind holds to be true.[6]

What do these liberal virtues require? Obviously, institutions that nurture public deliberation, including a free and responsible press and a faith in "objectivity" on the part of journalists. They require institutions of education that help citizens think for themselves and respect processes of self-exploration and intellectual inquiry. Academe marries the elite expectations of a liberal polity—for citizens to become public-minded, intelligent, thoughtful individuals—and the democratization of those virtues to as large a number of people as possible. That the conservative mind has waged war on academe throughout the years is telling, and it points to why a defense of education's role in creating democratic citizens is so necessary today.

Liberals must explain what virtues they believe in and then show why the things shouted down by conservatives—professionalism, science, academe, and journalistic objectivity—are necessary for a good society. This is not an easy task; it does not suit itself to the hype and yelling that define our public debate today. But that only makes these virtues all the more important to explain and champion, and it is why in today's political climate, liberals will likely become the party of order against the party of rebellion on the Right. Liberalism, no matter how much conservatives have ignored this point, has historically stood in the middle of the political spectrum; this was true even during the 1960s when liberals like Arthur Schlesinger Jr. and Richard Hofstadter condemned the violence of student protesters while also warning about a potential conservative backlash. Refusing to take up the extremes of either far Left or far Right, liberalism is a political theory that champions social order and civility. It appreciates just how fragile the civic life found in modern democracies really is.

Finally, I should offer a word about America's role in the world. This is not the right place to set out a liberal alternative to the Bush Doctrine or the war in Iraq. Plenty of writers have done that already. But this *is* the right place to state the obvious: liberals certainly believe in the use of American power abroad in the name of democratic principles, but they see the need to temper this with humility and realism. The appropriate balance between idealism—a faith that America can improve the world—and realism—a tempering of the type of optimism that can lead to dangerous extensions of power abroad—is a tough balance to strike. But the incessant bad news coming home from Iraq and the declining stature of America abroad make obvious today why we need to find the balance, especially as liberals argue against conservatives about foreign policy. And it also makes sense that liberals should lead the way. Liberals recognize the fragility of our civic fabric at home and the threat posed to it by conservative rebels, and they also appreciate the fragility of America's power abroad, especially evidenced in the neoconservative utopianism that drove the war in Iraq.

In the end, liberals must provide a vision of the country that offers an alternative to the one presented by the conservative mind. I cannot provide every element of that vision here. There's a history of liberalism that can help us here, and I have written about it elsewhere.[7] The strength of the conservative mind—which is drawn from its zeal and sense of apocalypse—requires liberals to explain what conservatives threaten to destroy when taking down liberalism. And here we get to a conundrum. Though it might falter, the conservative mind will not go away, but liberals also cannot fight the culture war the way conservatives do. David Horowitz might feel comfortable about dumping "rationality" for "political warfare" and Ann Coulter might love driving political opponents into an "impotent rage." But liberals can never do such things without violating their own first principles. Besides, liberals have a bigger responsibility—to point out what is lost when conservatives pursue culture wars at the expense of institutions and values that are so important to ensuring a democratic polity. To recognize the danger of the conservative mind's apocalyptic culture wars is the first step in that very important direction.

NOTES

Book Epigraph

Epigraph reference: David Riesman and Nathan Glazer, "The Intellectuals and Discontented Classes" (1955), in Daniel Bell, ed., *The Radical Right* (Garden City, N.Y.: Anchor Books, 1964), 133.

Introduction   The Party of Ideas?

Epigraph reference: Bush quoted in Robert A. George, "Guest Comment," *National Review Online*, August 4, 2000, posted at http://www.nationalreview.com/convention/guest_comment/guest_comment080400a.shtml.

1. Bush's "gut player" remark quoted in John Powers, *Sore Losers* (New York: Doubleday, 2004), 21; Jonathan Chait, "Race to the Bottom," *New Republic*, December 20, 1999, 26; Stephen Burd, "Bush's Next Target?" *Chronicle of Higher Education*, July 11, 2003, posted online; David Frum, *The Right Man* (New York: Random House, 2003), 272; on the book reading, see John Dickerson, "Stranger and Stranger: Why Is George Bush Reading Camus?" *Slate*, posted August 14, 2006.
2. Fred Barnes, *Rebel-in-Chief* (New York: Crown, 2006), 13, 14; John Podhoretz, *Bush Country: How Dubya Became a Great President While Driving Liberals Insane* (New York: St. Martin's, 2004).
3. Hitchens quoted in Ian Parker, "He Knew He Was Right," *New Yorker*, October 16, 2006, 157. Hitchens, of course, will never pledge complete support to the conservative movement owing to his unceasing atheism.
4. Nathan Glazer, "The Campus Crucible," in Mark Gerson, ed., *The Essential Neoconservative Reader* (Reading, Pa.: Addison, 1996), 46; John Powers, "Bubble Wrap," *LA Weekly*, August 30–September 5, 2002, read online; Brian C. Anderson, *South Park Conservatives* (Washington, D.C.: Regnery, 2005); Rod Dreher, *Crunchy Cons* (New York: Crown, 2006).
5. Academic Bill of Rights, posted at http://www.studentsforacademic-freedom.org/abor.html.

6. Phillip E. Johnson quoted in Stanley Fish, "Academic Cross-Dressing: How Intelligent Design Gets Its Arguments from the Left," *Harper's*, December 2005, 71.

7. Jeffrey Hart, *The Making of the American Conservative Mind* (Wilmington, Del.: ISI, 2005), 349; "*Idéologie* Has Taken Over," *Washington Monthly*, October 2006, 41.

8. John Dean, *Conservatives without Conscience* (New York: Viking, 2006), xi; Andrew Sullivan, *The Conservative Soul* (New York: Harper Collins, 2006), 5. See also here Christine Todd Whitman, *It's My Party Too* (New York: Penguin, 2005).

9. Coulter quoted in John Cloud, "Ms. Right," *Time*, April 25, 2005, 32–42. On Coulter's Deadhead past, see John Avlon, "Jerry Garcia's Conservative Children," *New York Sun*, August 9, 2005, online at http://www.nysun.com/article/18288.

10. Buckley quoted in John Judis, *William F. Buckley: Patron Saint of the Conservatives* (New York: Simon and Schuster, 1988), 97; William F. Buckley, *God and Man at Yale* (Chicago: Regnery, 1951), xvi.

11. Wechsler quoted in Dan Wakefield, "William F. Buckley: Portrait of a Complainer," *Esquire*, January 1961, 52.

12. Cloud, "Ms. Right." Coulter's action figure quotes are also from this article.

13. William Buckley and Brent Bozell, *McCarthy and His Enemies* (Chicago: Regnery, 1954), 310; Ann Coulter, *Treason: Liberal Treachery from the Cold War to the War on Terrorism* (New York: Crown Forum, 2003); Buckley, *Up from Liberalism* (New York: McDowell, 1959), 23; Ann Coulter, *Slander: Liberal Lies about the American Right* (New York: Crown, 2002), 91.

14. The classic work that defined the internal tensions of the conservative mind and that still merits reading today is George Nash, *The Conservative Intellectual Movement* (Wilmington, Del.: ISI, 1998). For an older work that develops the sense of "mind" that I use here, see W. J. Cash, *The Mind of the South* (1941; reprint, New York: Doubleday, 1954).

15. Arthur Schlesinger Jr., "Middle-Aged Man with a Horn," *New Republic*, March 16, 1953, 17; on Horowitz's comparison of himself to Chambers, see his *Radical Son* (New York: Free Press, 1997), 2.

16. Lionel Trilling, *The Liberal Imagination* (Garden City, N.Y.: Anchor Books, 1953), vii; Martin Sklar and James Weinstein, "Socialism and the New Left," *Studies on the Left* 6 (1966): 70. For more on the New Left interpretation of liberalism, see my "Between Despair and Hope: Revisiting Studies on the Left," in *The New Left Revisited*, ed. John McMillian and Paul Buhle (Philadelphia: Temple University Press, 2003).

17. John Crowe Ransom in *I'll Take My Stand* (1930; reprint, New York: Harper Torchbooks, 1962), 3, 1; Richard Pells, *Radical Visions and American Dreams* (New York: Harper and Row, 1973), 103; the

Southern Agrarians are also discussed in the next chapter. The intellectual who has most recuperated this tradition is Eugene Genovese in his *The Southern Tradition* (Cambridge: Harvard University Press, 1994).

18. Quoted in Judis, *William F. Buckley,* 140.

19. For an example of a recent treatment that overvalues Strauss's influence, see Earl Shorris, "Ignoble Liars: Leo Strauss, George Bush, and the Philosophy of Mass Deception," *Harper's,* June 2004, 65–71; and Shadia Drury, *Leo Strauss and the American Right* (New York: St. Martin's, 1997).

20. The most recent expression of this is Thomas Frank, *What's the Matter with Kansas?* (New York: Holt, 2004). The best intellectual history that emphasizes money and think tanks is Sidney Blumenthal, *The Rise of the Counter-Establishment* (New York: Harper and Row, 1988).

CHAPTER I   THE FIRST GENERATION

Epigraph reference: Frank Chodorov, "To the Editor: Controversy Begins," *National Review,* October 6, 1956, 23. Hereafter, *National Review* will be abbreviated in the notes as *NR*.

1. Daniel Bell, *The End of Ideology* (New York: Free Press, 1960), 393, 400.

2. Russell Kirk, *A Program for Conservatives* (Chicago: Regnery, 1954), 8.

3. Russell Kirk, "From the Academy: The Clutch of Ideology," *NR,* December 8, 1956, 13. For an interesting and thoughtful reflection on building a conservative ideology (the author thinks that it is too soon and too challenging), see Gerhart Niemeyer, "Too Early and Too Much," *NR,* October 13, 1956, 22–23.

4. William Buckley, "The Tranquil World of Dwight D. Eisenhower," *NR,* January 18, 1958, 57; Frank Meyer, "Principles and Heresies: On What Ball?" *NR,* January 4, 1958, 17; Meyer, "Calling All Intellectuals," reprinted in John Chamberlain, ed., *The National Review Reader* (New York: Bookmailer, 1957), 212. For more on these themes, see also Brent Bozell and Willmoore Kendall, "From the Democratic Convention," *NR,* August 25, 1956, 8; for Buckley on Eisenhower, see his "Mr. Eisenhower's Decision and the Eisenhower Program," in Chamberlain, *National Review Reader,* 187–189. For an interpretation of Ike as a closet liberal, see Brent Bozell, "National Trends: Why Mr. Rovere Likes Ike," *NR,* July 4, 1956, 7.

5. For a sense of this, see Kevin Smant, *Principles and Heresies: Frank S. Meyer and the Shaping of the American Conservative Movement* (Wilmington, Del.: ISI, 2002), 49.

6. James Burnham, "Should Conservatives Vote for Eisenhower-Nixon?: Yes," *NR,* October 20, 1956, 12, 14; William Schlamm,

"No," in ibid., 15; Brent Bozell, "Mr. Burnham's Missing Sanctions," *NR*, February 9, 1957, 127–128; on Chambers and Buckley, see the letters reprinted in William Buckley, ed., *Odyssey of a Friend* (New York: Putnam's, 1969). For Kirk's disagreement with Buckley, see Kirk's *Academic Freedom* (Chicago: Regnery, 1955) and for Chambers's disagreement, see later in this chapter.

7. For a classic statement on conservatives and the Cold War, see Frank Meyer, "Principles and Heresies: The Concept of Fortress America," *NR*, April 26, 1958. Here Meyer writes: "There are no international struggles from which we can isolate ourselves; there is only the struggle between the Soviet Union and us" (400).

8. James Burnham, "The Third World War: The Answer to Sputniks," *NR*, December 14, 1957, 542.

9. "National Trends: Why the Moon Is Red II," *NR*, November 2, 1957, 392.

10. Sam Tannenhaus, *Whittaker Chambers* (New York: Random House, 1997), 450.

11. Whittaker Chambers, *Witness* (1952; reprint, Washington, D.C.: Regnery, 2002), 12.

12. James Burnham, *Suicide of the West* (New Rochelle, N.Y.: Arlington, 1975), 291.

13. Willmoore Kendall, "Three on the Line," *NR*, August 31, 1957, 181.

14. Eugene Lyons, "The Anatomy of Neutralism," *NR*, July 18, 1956, 9.

15. "I Acknowledge My Mistakes," in Chamberlain, *National Review Reader*, 46–47.

16. Bernard DeVoto, *The Easy Chair* (Boston: Houghton Mifflin, 1955), 177; Chambers, *Witness*, 209.

17. Arthur Schlesinger Jr., "Middle-aged Man with a Horn," *New Republic*, March 16, 1953, 17. John Patrick Diggins explored this theme in his important book, *Up from Communism* (New York: Harper and Row, 1975).

18. Lionel Trilling, *The Middle of the Journey* (1947; reprint, New York: Avon, 1966), 119.

19. For some reflections on this idea, see Martin Jay, *Marxism and Totality* (Berkeley: University of California Press, 1984).

20. James Burnham, *The Coming Defeat of Communism* (New York: J. Day, 1950), 61.

21. Whittaker Chambers, "Books in Review: Big Sister Is Watching You," *NR*, December 28, 1957, 596.

22. Kathleen Morris in "To the Editor: To the Chamber, Chambers!" *NR*, January 18, 1958, 71; Kevin Coughlin in "To the Editor," *NR*, February 1, 1958, 119. On this conflict between Chambers and Rand, see Jennifer Burns, "Godless Capitalism: Ayn Rand and the Conservative Movement," *Modern Intellectual History* 1, 3 (2004): 1–27.

23. Peter Viereck, *Conservatism Revisited* (New York: Free Press, 1962), 38, 32 (these quotes come from the reprinted 1949 book); Viereck quoted in George Nash, *The Conservative Intellectual Movement* (Wilmington, Del.: ISI, 1998), 142; Meyer quoted in ibid., 142; Frank Meyer, "Principles and Heresies: Other-Directed Champion of Other-Directed Court," *NR*, August 24, 1957, 160.

24. Chambers, *Witness*, 472; Rusher quoted in Nash, *Conservative Intellectual Movement*, 137; Burnham, *Suicide of the West*, 297; "Confidential: Among Ourselves," *NR*, December 1, 1956, 17, 15–16.

25. John Judis, *William F. Buckley: Patron Saint of the Conservatives* (New York: Simon and Schuster, 1988), 29, 38, 39, 58.

26. Ibid., 12. For the WASP culture of Yale, see for instance, Geoffrey Kabaservice, *The Guardians: Kingman Brewster, His Circle, and the Rise of the Liberal Establishment* (New York: Henry Holt, 2004), 13.

27. William F. Buckley, *God and Man at Yale* (Chicago: Regnery, 1951), xiv. Hereafter, all references to this work will be cited parenthetically in the text by page number.

28. Judis, *William F. Buckley*, 86.

29. Barton quoted in William Buckley, *Miles Gone By: A Literary Autobiography* (Washington, D.C.: Regnery, 2004), 76–77.

30. Garry Wills once said that Wilmoore Kendall was the "only anti-elitist at *National Review* in the 1950s." Garry Wills, *Confessions of a Conservative* (Garden City, N.Y.: Doubleday, 1979), 24. That's not exactly right. After all, Kendall was Buckley's teacher. Most seem to think that Buckley was split between a populist leaning and an elitist leaning. Kendall had profound impact on Buckley, and Kendall was certainly a populist (see Nash, *Conservative Intellectual Movement*, 231). See also Jeffrey Hart, *The Making of the Conservative Mind: National Review and Its Times* (Wilmington, Del.: ISI, 2005), 14.

31. Dwight Macdonald, "Scrambled Eggheads," *Commentary*, April 1956, 368; Macdonald also quoted in Michael Wreszin, *A Rebel in Defense of Tradition* (New York: Basic Books, 1994), 274; Macdonald quoted in Judis, *William F. Buckley*, 97; Gregory Schneider, *Cadres for Conservatism: Young Americans for Freedom and the Rise of the Contemporary Right* (New York: New York University Press, 1999), 14.

32. See here George Cotkin, *Existential America* (Baltimore: Johns Hopkins University Press, 2003).

33. John Patrick Diggins, *The Proud Decades* (New York: Norton, 1989), 197–198.

34. M. Stanton Evans, *Revolt on Campus* (Chicago: Regnery, 1961), 7; Judis, *William F. Buckley*, 75, 184.

35. "The Ivory Tower: Has History Tenure?" *NR*, April 5, 1958, 328. See also Buckley, "The Ivory Tower: As for the Nonconformists," *NR*, March 16, 1957, 261.

36. Quoted in Richard Fried, *Nightmare in Red: The McCarthy Era in Perspective* (New York: Oxford University Press, 1990), 123.
37. Judis, *William F. Buckley*, 110; William Buckley and L. Brent Bozell, *McCarthy and His Enemies* (Chicago: Regnery, 1954), 305–306.
38. Chambers in Buckley, *Odyssey of a Friend*, 52, 102.
39. Bozell, "National Trends: 'This Was a Man,'" *NR*, May 18, 1957, 468.
40. Buckley and Bozell, *McCarthy and His Enemies*, 62, 310.
41. Diggins, *Up from Communism*, 439.
42. "The End of McCarthy," *NR*, May 18, 1957, 462.
43. Frank Meyer, "Principles and Heresies: The Meaning of McCarthyism," *NR*, June 14, 1958, 565, 566.
44. William Schlamm, "Across McCarthy's Grave," *NR*, May 18, 1957, 470.
45. Howe quoted in Neil Jumonville, ed., *The New York Intellectuals Reader* (New York: Routledge, 2007), 2. See Paul Gottfried, *The Conservative Movement* (New York: Twayne, 1993), 11.
46. William F. Buckley, "*National Review*: Statement of Intentions," in Gregory Schneider, ed., *Conservatism in America since 1930: A Reader* (New York: New York University Press, 2003), 195, 196, 198, 199; Buckley, "*National Review*: Credenda and Statement of Principles," in ibid., 201, 202, 203.
47. John Chamberlain, "The New Journalism," *NR*, April 6, 1957, 329.
48. Mary Reisner, "To the Editor," *NR*, December 1, 1956, 22.
49. "Professorial" from John Judis, *Grand Illusion* (New York: Farrar Straus Giroux, 1992), 150.
50. John Leonard, "The Black Album," *New York Review of Books*, October 20, 2005, read online. On Didion's western politics, see Mark Royden Winchell, *Joan Didion* (New York: Twayne, 1980), 37.
51. Nathan Glazer in Mark Gerson, ed., *The Essential Neoconservative Reader* (Reading, Mass.: Addison-Wesley, 1996), 46. E. J. Dionne Jr. has pointed to a connection in style between Buckley and the New Left; see his *Why Americans Hate Politics* (New York: Simon and Schuster, 1991), 159. Priscilla Buckley, *Living It Up with* National Review (Dallas: Spence, 2005) provides a good sense of the internal operations of the magazine.
52. Quoted in Judis, *William F. Buckley*, 140.
53. Edmund Burke, *Reflections on the Revolution in France* (New York: Liberal Arts Press, 1955), 99.
54. Whittaker Chambers, *Cold Friday* (New York: Random House, 1964), 7.
55. Kirk, *Program for Conservatives*, 3.
56. Russell Kirk, "From the Academy: Babbitt Read Anew," *NR*, January 19, 1957, 67.
57. The "anti-intellectualism of the intellectuals" has been identified on the Left, but it is clearly stronger on the Right. For the idea of the

"anti-intellectualism of the intellectuals," see Christopher Lasch, *The New Radicalism in America: The Intellectual as a Social Type* (New York: Norton, 1965).

58. Quotes here from Richard Hofstadter, *Anti-Intellectualism in American Life* (New York: Vintage, 1963), 9–10.

59. See here George Cotkin, "The Tragic Predicament: Postwar American Intellectuals, Acceptance, and Mass Culture," in Jeremy Jenning and Anthony Kemp-Welch, eds., *Intellectuals in Politics: From the Dreyfus Affair to Salman Rushdie* (London: Routledge, 1997).

60. Russell Kirk, *The Conservative Mind* (Chicago: Regnery, 1953), 309, 297.

61. Kirk, *Program for Conservatives*, 20, 34–35, 87.

62. Richard Weaver, "Roots of the Liberal Complacency," *NR*, June 8, 1957, 542, 543.

63. Russell Kirk, *Randolph of Roanoke* (Chicago: Regnery, 1951), 3, 63; Kirk, *Conservative Mind*, 132, 149–157. For more on Kirk's biography, see W. Wesley McDonald, *Russell Kirk and the Age of Ideology* (Columbia: University of Missouri Press, 2004), 19.

64. For Weaver's life, I rely on Fred Young, *Richard M. Weaver* (Columbia: University of Missouri Press, 1995), and the essays gathered in Joseph Scotchie, ed., *The Vision of Richard Weaver* (New Brunswick, N.J.: Transaction Books, 1995).

65. Twelve Southerners, *I'll Take My Stand* (1930; reprint, New York: Harper Torchbooks, 1962), 7, xxiv.

66. Richard Weaver, *Ideas Have Consequences* (Chicago: University of Chicago Press, 1948), 3, 130.

67. Ibid., 55; Richard Weaver, "The Regime of the South," *NR*, March 14, 1959, 588.

68. Tate quoted in Mark Malvasi, *The Unregenerate South* (Baton Rouge: Louisiana State University Press, 1997), 17. It should be pointed out that some conservatives were more content to locate conservative principles in natural law rather than a historically rooted society: See for instance, Frank Meyer, "Principles and Heresies: The Relativist 'Re-evaluates' Evil," *NR*, May 4, 1957, 429.

69. Gavin Wright, *Old South/New South* (New York: Basic Books, 1986), 50.

70. W. J. Cash, *The Mind of the South* (1941; reprint, New York: Doubleday, 1954), 43–44, 305.

71. Willmoore Kendall, "How to Read Richard Weaver," *Intercollegiate Review*, September 1965, 82.

72. Richard Whalen, "Rural Virginia: A Microcosm," *NR*, March 8, 1958, 231.

73. Richard Weaver, "Books in Review: Integration Is Communization," *NR*, July 13, 1957, 67, 68.

74. Richard Weaver, "The Lincoln-Douglas Debates," *NR*, June 21, 1958, 18–19.
75. "The Assault on Ms. Lucy," in Chamberlain, *National Review Reader*, 254; "Voices of Sanity," in ibid., 263; "The Tank as Educator," in ibid., 264–265; see also "The South Girds Its Loins" in the same collection. For more on this context, see chapter 1 of Carol Polsgrove, *Divided Minds: Intellectuals and the Civil Rights Movement* (New York: Norton, 2001). Faulkner's quote about "shooting Negroes" can be found in Polsgrove on 15.
76. "Why the South Must Prevail," *NR*, August 24, 1957, 149.
77. "Open Question," *NR*, September 7, 1957, 209. On Faubus, see Brent Bozell, "National Trends: Governor Faubus Clouds the Issue," *NR*, September 21, 1957, 248.
78. James Jackson Kilpatrick, "Right and Power in Arkansas," *NR*, September 28, 1957, 275.
79. "The Lie to Mr. Eisenhower," *NR*, October 5, 1957, 293.
80. "Bayonets and the Law," *NR*, October 12, 1957, 317.
81. "Principles and Heresies: The Constitutional Crisis," *NR*, October 26, 1957, 378.
82. Anthony Harrigan, "The South Is Different," *NR*, March 8, 1958, 226, 227.
83. Jonathan Mitchell, "Why the South Likes Lausche," *NR*, May 23, 1956, 15.
84. For more on this point, see my essay, "Liberalism and Democracy: A Troubled Marriage," in Neil Jumonville and Kevin Mattson, eds., *Liberalism for a New Century* (Berkeley: University of California Press, 2007).
85. For a prescient view on this, see "Southern Republican Blues," *NR*, May 3, 1958, 425.
86. "The Young Grow Up," *NR*, April 27, 1957, 393–394; this was repeated in "Younger Statesmen," *NR*, July 6, 1957, 31.
87. "The Ivory Tower: The Case for Silence," *NR*, March 29, 1958, 306.
88. Richard Pells, *The Liberal Mind in a Conservative Age* (Middletown, Conn.: Wesleyan University Press, 1989), 186.
89. Kirk, *Conservative Mind*, 428; Kirk, *Program for Conservatives*, 207; Kirk, *Beyond the Dreams of Avarice* (Chicago: Regnery, 1956), ix.
90. Richard Weaver, "Roots of the Liberal Complacency," *NR*, June 8, 1957, 541, 543. It should be pointed out that this sort of individualistic rebellion was also the sort that William Whyte hoped for in the end to his book, *The Organization Man* (New York: Doubleday, 1957), 443–448.
91. Buckley, "The Decline of Partisanship," *NR*, February 14, 1959, 527.
92. Frank Meyer, "Principles and Heresies: McCarthy's Unforfeited Word," *NR*, June 8, 1957, 548.
93. See Russell Kirk, "From the Academy: The Federal Educational Boondoggle," *NR*, March 22, 1958, 257.

94. Frank Meyer, "Principles and Heresies: Norman Mailer's Culture Hero," *NR*, July 27, 1957, 113.
95. Kirk, *Conservative Mind*, 401.
96. Quoted in Judis, *William F. Buckley*, 169.

CHAPTER 2   THE BIG CHILL THAT SET FIRES

Epigraph reference: Russell Kirk, "The University and Revolution: An Insane Conjunction," *Intercollegiate Review* (Winter 1969): 18.

 1. Morris Dickstein, *Gates of Eden: American Culture in the Sixties* (New York: Basic Books, 1977); Ronald Berman, *America in the Sixties: An Intellectual History* (New York: Colophon, 1968), 209; and more recently Marianne DeKoven, *Utopia Limited: The Sixties and the Emergence of the Postmodern* (Durham, N.C.: Duke University Press, 2004).
 2. M. Stanton Evans, *Revolt on the Campus* (Chicago: Regnery, 1961), 34, 231, 240; M. Stanton Evans, "The Ivory Tower: Notes on a Liberal Love Feast," *NR*, March 16, 1957, 260; Port Huron Statement, as reprinted in James Miller, *Democracy Is in the Streets* (New York: Simon and Schuster, 1987), 329.
 3. M. Stanton Evans, *The Liberal Establishment* (New York: Devin-Adair, 1965), especially 54–56; journalist quoted in John Andrews, *The Other Side of the Sixties* (New Brunswick, N.J.: Rutgers University Press, 1997), 147.
 4. Andrews, *Other Side of the Sixties*, 26, 30; Gregory Schneider, *Cadres for Conservatism* (New York: New York University Press, 1999), 33.
 5. Buckley quoted in Schneider, *Cadres for Conservatism*, 32.
 6. See here Rick Perlstein, *Before the Storm* (New York: Hill and Wang, 2001); Matthew Dallek, *The Right Moment* (New York: Free Press, 2000); Lisa McGirr, *Suburban Warriors* (Princeton, N.J.: Princeton University Press, 2001). For more on the youthfulness of Goldwater campaign workers, see William Rickenbacker, "Looking Up," *NR*, May 5, 1964, 354.
 7. Brent Bozell, "The 1958 Elections: Coroner's Report," *NR*, November 22, 1958, 335; Bozell, "Comes the Dawn," *NR*, May 7, 1963, 345; see also Bozell's optimism about Barry Goldwater in "Death Throes of a Proud Party," *NR*, January 31, 1959, 487.
 8. See Schneider, *Cadres for Conservatism*, 27.
 9. Barry Goldwater, *The Conscience of a Conservative* (Shepherdsville, Ky.: Victor, 1960).
10. Frank Meyer, "Principles and Heresies: Conservatism and the Goldwater Consensus," *NR*, November 5, 1963, 386.
11. Perlstein, *Before the Storm*, 268, 266.
12. Quoted in Perlstein, *Before the Storm*, 315, 360; Barry Goldwater, "Opening Campaign Speech," in Richard Hofstadter, ed., *Great Issues in American History* (New York: Vintage, 1982), 502.

13. Speech quoted in Perlstein, *Before the Storm,* 391.
14. "*NR* and Goldwater," *NR,* January 14, 1964, 9.
15. "Goldwater's Tribulations: The Press," *NR,* June 9, 1964 (review bulletin), 1.
16. Evans, *Liberal Establishment,* 50.
17. Russell Kirk, "From the Academy: The Campus Conservative Journals," *NR,* June 2, 1964, 449.
18. Mario Savio, "An End to History" (1964), reprinted in Alexander Bloom and Wini Breines, eds., *Takin' It to the Streets* (New York: Oxford University Press, 2003), 92.
19. Angelo Codevilla, "Why the Discontent on Campus," *Intercollegiate Review* (March–April 1966): 326. Hereafter, this publication will be abbreviated *IR* in the notes.
20. David Greenwald, "The Ideology of the New Left: An Interpretation," *IR* (September–October 1966): 17.
21. Sam Kaplan, "Correspondence: The New Left, Anarchy, and Marxism," *IR* (January–February 1967): 141.
22. Noam Chomsky, *American Power and the New Mandarins* (New York: Pantheon, 1969), 26, 53.
23. Albert Hobbs, "The Falseface of Science," *IR* (January 1965): 22.
24. Francis Wilson, "The Revolt of the Sophists," *IR* (November–December 1966): 67.
25. M. Stanton Evans, "The New Totalitarians," *IR* (Spring 1969): 160.
26. John Stassen, "The Rhetoric of Student Revolt," *IR* (November–December 1965): 200, 204.
27. Codevilla, "Why the Discontent on Campus," 323, 324.
28. Evans, "New Totalitarians," 162, 163.
29. Donald Atwell Zoll, "Violence in the Civilized Society," *IR* (Fall 1968): 6; Albert Hobbs, "The SDS Trip," *IR* (Spring 1969): 148, 155.
30. Russell Kirk, "The University and Revolution," *IR* (Winter 1969–1970): 13, 16; Eliseo Vivas, "Herbert Marcuse," *IR* (Winter 1969–1970): 66; Schneider, *Cadres for Conservatism,* 116, 135; Antoni Gollan, "The Great Marijuana Problem," *NR,* January 30, 1968, 79.
31. *NR,* May 7, 1968, 468.
32. See Schneider, *Cadres for Conservatism,* 110–111.
33. There are numerous books on the New York intellectuals. See Neil Jumonville, *Critical Crossings* (Berkeley: University of California Press, 1991); Alexander Bloom, *The New York Intellectuals and Their World* (New York: Oxford University Press, 1986); and Terry Cooney, *The Rise of the New York Intellectuals* (Madison: University of Wisconsin Press, 1986).
34. It is not clear when exactly the term "neoconservative" entered the American political lexicon. It might have been an offhand comment by Michael Harrington in 1972. A democratic socialist activist and

intellectual, Harrington shared with Irving Kristol and Norman Podhoretz a disgust with the New Left's confrontational politics and the counterculture's cult of self-exploration. But Harrington chafed at Kristol's hardening critique of the welfare state and drift toward Richard Nixon's presidency, two characteristics that suggested a "new conservatism" on the rise. The term "new conservative" continued to be heard in democratic leftist circles for numerous years, culminating in *The New Conservatives: A Critique from the Left*, a book edited by Irving Howe and released in 1974. But it was not until 1976 that the term "gained a certain degree of currency" and was "accepted good-humoredly by some adherents of the viewpoint," as Peter Steinfels points out. Nonetheless, even if the term was not in wide circulation by the mid-1960s, its broad outlines were already clear by then. For the quotes above, see Maurice Isserman, *The Other American: The Life of Michael Harrington* (New York: Public Affairs, 2000), 304–305; Peter Steinfels, *The Neoconservatives: The Men Who Are Changing America's Politics* (New York: Simon and Schuster, 1979), 2.

35. Nathan Glazer, "Towards an Imperial Judiciary," *Public Interest* (Fall 1975): 104–123; on the press, see Paul Weaver, "The New Journalism and the Old," *Public Interest* (Spring 1974): 89–120; and Samuel Harrington, "The Democratic Distemper," *Public Interest* (Fall 1975): 23–38.

36. Nathan Glazer's "anti-institutional" remark is in "The New Left and Its Limits," *Commentary* (July 1968): 38; see also Diana Trilling, "On the Steps of Low Library," *Commentary* (November 1968): 29–55; Robert Nisbet, "The Future of the University," *Commentary* (February 1971): 62–71. On Kristol's doubts about academic freedom, see William F. Buckley, *Miles Gone By* (Washington, D.C.: Regnery, 2004), 85.

37. Daniel Bell, "Notes on the Post-Industrial Society (I)," *Public Interest* (Winter 1967): 27; and "Notes on the Post-Industrial Society (II)," *Public Interest* (Spring 1967): 102.

38. James Burnham, "The Managerial Revolution," *Partisan Review* (May–June 1941): 190.

39. See Gary Dorrien, *The Neoconservative Mind: Politics, Culture, and the War of Ideology* (Philadelphia: Temple University Press, 1993), 382.

40. Colin Clark, "The Horrible Proposals of Mr. Galbraith," *NR*, October 11, 1958, 238. On Galbraith's thought, see Richard Pells, *The Liberal Mind in a Conservative Age* (Middletown, Conn.: Wesleyan University Press, 1989), 172.

41. Irving Kristol, *Two Cheers for Capitalism* (New York: Basic Books, 1978), 183.

42. Irving Kristol, "New Left, New Right," *Public Interest* (Summer 1966): 6.

43. Irving Kristol, *Neoconservatism: The Autobiography of an Idea* (New York: Free Press, 1995), 381.

44. Maurice Isserman and Michael Kazin, *America Divided* (New York: Oxford University Press, 2000), 245.

45. For a fine account of the rise of the religious Right that highlights its relation to liberalism, see Jason Bivins, *The Fracture of Good Order: Christian Antiliberalism and the Challenge to American Politics* (Chapel Hill: University of North Carolina Press, 2003), chap. 3.

46. Irving Kristol, " 'Civil Liberties,' 1952—A Study in Confusion," *Commentary* (March 1952): 229.

47. See Dorrien, *Neoconservative Mind,* 77–78.

48. Kristol, *Two Cheers for Capitalism,* 134.

49. Kristol, *Neoconservatism,* 204, 351.

50. Kristol, *Two Cheers for Capitalism,* 7; and on the new class and populism, see 27–28.

51. Irving Kristol, *On the Democratic Idea in America* (New York: Harper and Row, 1972), 4.

52. Sidney Blumenthal, *The Rise of the Counter-Establishment: From Conservative Ideology to Political Power* (New York: Harper and Row, 1988), 148.

53. Podhoretz's marriage is nicely detailed in his wife's book: Midge Decter, *An Old Wife's Tale* (New York: Regan Books, 2001), 43–45.

54. Norman Podhoretz, "Introduction" and "The Young Generation" (1957) in *Doings and Undoings: The Fifties and After in American Writing* (New York: Farrar, Straus and Giroux, 1966), 8, 111. For autobiographical details here, I rely on Jumonville, *Critical Crossings,* 188–200.

55. Norman Podhoretz, "Know-Nothing Bohemians" (1958), in Thomas Jeffers, ed., *The Norman Podhoretz Reader* (New York: Free Press, 2004), 32, 35, 37.

56. Paul Goodman, *Growing Up Absurd* (New York: Random House, 1960), 280.

57. Carl Rollyson, *The Lives of Norman Mailer* (New York: Paragon, 1991), 128.

58. Norman Mailer, *Advertisements for Myself* (New York: Signet, 1959), 15, 284.

59. Podhoretz, *Doings and Undoings,* 367.

60. Podhoretz's writing about New York intellectuals in gossipy terms has now become a new prism through which to see this group's work as a whole. See David Laskin, *Partisans: Marriage, Politics, and Betrayal among the New York Intellectuals* (New York: Simon and Schuster, 2000).

61. Norman Podhoretz, *Making It* (New York: Random House, 1967), 53, 146, 202.

62. Podhoretz, *Making It,* 356; Norman Podhoretz, *Breaking Ranks* (New York: Harper and Row, 1979), 222; Norman Podhoretz, "Vietnam and Collective Guilt," *Commentary* (March 1973): 4; Podhoretz quoted in Blumenthal, *Rise of the Counter-establishment,* 138.

63. Norman Podhoretz, *The Present Danger: "Do We Have the Will to Reverse the Decline of American Power?"* (New York: Simon and Schuster, 1980), 30, 76, 79; Norman Podhoretz, "Making the World Safe for Communism," *Commentary* (April 1976): 35.

64. Dan T. Carter, *The Politics of Rage: George Wallace, the Origins of the New Conservatism, and the Transformation of American Politics* (New York: Simon and Schuster, 1995), 299.

65. Kevin Phillips, "Revolutionary Music," *Washington Post,* May 6, 1971, A19; Kevin Phillips, *The Emerging Republican Majority* (New Rochelle, N.Y.: Arlington House, 1969), especially 461–462; for more on Phillips, see Alan Crawford, *Thunder on the Right: The "New Right" and the Politics of Resentment* (New York: Pantheon, 1980), 182–186; and Michael Kazin, *The Populist Persuasion* (Ithaca, N.Y.: Cornell University Press, 1998), 251.

66. Kevin Phillips, "Political Responses to the New Class," in B. Bruce-Briggs, ed., *The New Class?* (New York: McGraw-Hill, 1981), 140, 142.

67. Jeane Kirkpatrick, "Why the New Right Lost," *Commentary* (February 1977): 39.

68. Glazer quoted in Murray Friedman, *The Neoconservative Revolution* (Cambridge: Cambridge University Press, 2005), 235.

69. Damon Linker, *The Theocons* (New York: Doubleday, 2006), 58.

70. Norman Podhoretz, *My Love Affair with America* (New York: Free Press, 2000), 205, 208.

CHAPTER 3   POSTMODERN CONSERVATISM, THE POLITICS OF OUTRAGE, AND THE MINDSET OF WAR

Epigraph reference: David Horowitz, *The Art of Political War and Other Radical Pursuits* (Dallas, Tex.: Spence, 2000), 10.

1. The description of Horowitz is in Sidney Blumenthal, "Second Thoughts," in *Our Long National Daydream* (New York: Harper Collins, 1988), 251. I also rely on David Horowitz, *Radical Son* (New York: Free Press, 1997) for details about his life. On page 2 of that book he compares himself to Whittaker Chambers by describing himself as "the most hated ex-radical of my generation." For another version of this comparison, see John Podhoretz, "Journey Round His Father," *Weekly Standard*, March 17, 1997, 30–33.

2. Kramer quoted in Blumenthal, "Second Thoughts," 254.

3. Paglia quoted in Horowitz, *The Art of Political War*, 96.

4. David Horowitz, *The Art of Political War: How Republicans Can Fight to Win*, in *Left Illusions* (Dallas: Spence, 2003), 360, 356. This pamphlet, an excerpt from Horowitz's book by the same title, was distributed to "thirty-five state Republican Party chairmen [who] have endorsed it," and then "House majority whip Tom DeLay provided copies to every Republican Congressional officeholder, with a cover

note praising its contents." Scott Sherman, "David Horowitz's Long March," *Nation,* July 3, 2000, 12.

5. Peter Collier and David Horowitz, *Destructive Generation: Second Thoughts about the Sixties* (New York: Summit Books, 1990), 364.

6. Morris Dickstein, *Gates of Eden* (New York: Basic Books, 1977), 248; Theodore Roszak, *The Making of a Counterculture* (1968; reprint, Berkeley: University of California Press, 1995), 205, 227, 207.

7. Albert Borgmann, *Crossing the Postmodern Divide* (Chicago: University of Chicago Press, 1992), 55, 57; John Patrick Diggins, *The Rise and Fall of the American Left* (New York: Norton, 1992), 347.

8. Mark Lilla, *The Reckless Mind: Intellectuals in Politics* (New York: New York Review of Books, 2001), 186–187.

9. Michel Foucault, *Power/Knowledge* (New York: Pantheon, 1980), 126. On Foucault's fascination with the Iranian revolution, see Janet Afary and Kevin Anderson, *Foucault and the Iranian Revolution* (Chicago: University of Chicago Press, 2005).

10. Paul Weyrich, "Blue Collar or Blue Blood?: The New Right Compared with the Old Right," in Robert Whitaker, ed., *The New Right Papers* (New York: St. Martin's, 1982), 50.

11. See on this point, see Mary Brennan, *Turning Right in the Sixties* (Chapel Hill: University of North Carolina Press, 1995), 142.

12. Damon Linker, *The Theocons: Secular America under Siege* (New York: Doubleday, 2006); see also my review, "Attacking Secular America," *Dissent* (Winter 2007): 139–141.

13. See especially Todd Gitlin, *The Twilight of Common Dreams* (New York: Metropolitan, 1995).

14. I should make clear that this tendency is mirrored on the Left in the work of Al Franken and Michael Moore. For more on this point, see my "The Perils of Michael Moore," *Dissent* (Spring 2003): 75–81.

15. Ann Coulter, *Slander* (New York: Crown, 2002), 197; Coulter, *How to Talk to a Liberal (if You Must)* (New York: Crown Forum, 2004), 37, 10.

16. David Gilson, "Michael Savage's Long, Strange Trip," Salon.com, March 5, 2003.

17. Michael Savage, *Liberalism Is a Mental Disorder* (Nashville, Tenn.: Nelson Current, 2005), xx, xxvi.

18. Hanna Rosin, "Oedipus and Podhoretz," *New York,* January 5, 1998, read online at http://nymag.com.

19. Theodor Adorno, "On the Fetish Character in Music and the Regression of Listening," in Andrew Arato and Eike Gebhardt, eds., *The Essential Frankfurt School Reader* (New York: Continuum, 1985), 286, 292, 274.

20. Penley and Twitchell quoted in Thomas Frank, *One Market under God* (New York: Doubleday, 2000), 301, 296; Robert Venturi,

Denise Scott Brown, and Stephen Izenour, *Learning from Las Vegas* (Cambridge: MIT Press, 1972); see also Andreas Huyssen, *After the Great Divide: Modernism, Mass Culture, Postmodernism* (Bloomington: Indiana University Press, 1986); and David Harvey, *The Condition of Postmodernity* (Oxford: Basil Blackwell, 1990), 60.

21. For more on this, see Brian Anderson, *South Park Conservatives* (Washington, D.C.: Regnery, 2005).
22. Fred Barnes, "In Praise of Highways," *Weekly Standard*, April 27, 1998, 15. Hereafter, *Weekly Standard* will be abbreviated in the notes as *WS*.
23. Fred Barnes, "Suburban Beauty," *WS*, May 22, 2000, 28.
24. Charles Krauthammer, "The Decline of Baseball Civilization," *WS*, April 13, 1998, 27.
25. Michael Anton, "The Hyper-Entertaining of America," *WS*, April 15, 1996, 21, 23.
26. David Brooks, ed., *Backward and Upward* (New York: Vintage, 1995), xii.
27. David Brooks, "Love, American Style," *WS*, July 3/July 10, 2000 (double issue), 37.
28. David Brooks, *Bobos in Paradise* (New York: Simon and Schuster, 2000), 150; and Brooks's review of Podhoretz's work in his "Love, American Style," 36–37.
29. David Brooks, "Among the Bourgeoisophobes," *WS*, April 15, 2002, 21.
30. David Brooks, *On Paradise Drive* (New York: Simon and Schuster, 2004), 73, 70; *Bobos in Paradise* 61; *On Paradise Drive*, 70, 71.
31. Brooks, *On Paradise Drive*, 130.
32. Ibid., 207.
33. Ibid., 196.
34. Ibid., 208, 211, 279.
35. Quoted in "Iconoclastic Weekly Grabs Attention on the Right," *New York Times*, May 23, 1996, B12.
36. David Carr, "White House Listens When Weekly Speaks," *New York Times*, March 11, 2003, E1.
37. Robert Kagan and William Kristol, "What to Do about Iraq," *WS*, January 21, 2002, 23–26.
38. Lawrence Kaplan and William Kristol, *The War over Iraq* (San Francisco: Encounter, 2003), 125; see also David Frum and Richard Perle, *An End to Evil* (New York: Random House, 2003).
39. Fred Barnes, *Rebel-in-Chief* (New York: Crown, 2006), 13, 14; John Podhoretz, *Bush Country: How Dubya Became a Great President While Driving Liberals Insane* (New York: St. Martin's, 2004).
40. Podhoretz, *Bush Country*, 1.
41. See for instance "Bush's Iraq Legacy," *WS*, November 20, 2006, 9–11.

42. Horowitz quoted in Stanley Fish, "'Intellectual Diversity': The Trojan Horse of a Dark Design," *Chronicle of Higher Education*, February 13, 2004, B14.

43. For a fine overview of this history, see Michael Berube, *What's Liberal about the Liberal Arts?* (New York: Norton, 2006), chap. 2.

44. William Buckley, "The Ivory Tower: Here Lies the Empty Mind," *NR*, April 20, 1957, 382.

45. Academic Bill of Rights, posted at http://www.studentsforacademic-freedom.org/abor.html.

46. Ibid.

47. For more on this, see my "A Student Bill of Fights," *Nation*, April 4, 2005, 16–17.

48. Quoted in "Avoid Whatever Offends You," *Inside Higher Education*, February 17, 2006 (online).

49. Quoted in Jeffrey Brainard et al., "GOP Looks to Put Its Mark on Higher Education," *Chronicle of Higher Education*, November 12, 2004, A11.

50. Larry Mumper quoted in Joe Hallett, "Right-Winger's Bill to Stifle Campus Left-Leaners Is a Surefire Backfire," *Columbus Dispatch*, January 30, 2005.

51. Frank Meyer, "Principles and Heresies: The Bigotry of Science," *NR*, March 8, 1958, 234; see also Albert Hobbs, "The Falseface of Science," *Intercollegiate Review* (January 1965): 17–22.

52. Whittaker Chambers, *Witness* (1952; reprint, Washington, D.C.: Regnery, 2002), 19, 16.

53. Roszak, *Making of a Counterculture*, 205, 258; Howard Brick, *The Age of Contradiction* (Ithaca, N.Y.: Cornell University Press, 1998), 116.

54. Andrew Ferguson, "How Steven Pinker's Mind Works," *WS*, January 12, 1998, 16–24.

55. Quote of the Wedge Document in Chris Mooney, *The Republican War on Science* (New York: Basic Books, 2005), 173.

56. For more on this history, see Michael Ruse, "Liberalism, Science, and Evolution," in Neil Jumonville and Kevin Mattson, eds., *Liberalism for a New Century* (Berkeley: University of California Press, 2007).

57. Barbara Forrest and Paul Gross, *Creationism's Trojan Horse: The Wedge of Intelligent Design* (New York: Oxford University Press, 2004), 240–241.

58. Bush quoted in Linker, *Theocons*, 187.

59. Jodi Wilgoven, "Politicized Scholars Put Evolution on Defensive," *New York Times*, August 21, 2005, 1.

60. Quoted in Stanley Fish, "Academic Cross-Dressing: How Intelligent Design Gets Its Arguments from the Left," *Harper's*, December 2005, 71.

61. See for instance, M. Stanton Evans, "At Home," *NR*, January 21, 1964 (bulletin), 6.

62. Agnew quoted in Chris Lehmann, "The Eyes of Spiro are upon You," *The Baffler*, no. 14 (2001): 27.

63. Edith Efron, *The News Twisters* (Los Angeles: Nash, 1971), 19, 68, 132, 142, 168. Quote about agreeing with the press comes from 27.

64. "Statement of Intentions," in Gregory Schneider, ed., *Conservatism in America since 1930* (New York: New York University Press, 2003), 198. Wolfe quoted in Brick, *Age of Contradiction,* 38. For more on new journalism, see Marc Weingarten, *The Gang That Wouldn't Write Straight* (New York: Crown, 2006).

65. Judith Regan quoted in Paula Span, "Making Books: The Politics of Publishing," *Washington Post*, Book World, November 6, 2005, posted online.

66. See Michael Massing, "The End of News?" *New York Review of Books*, December 1, 2005, 23–27.

67. Andrew Ferguson, "Media-Bashing, Liberal Style," *WS*, January 29, 1996, 39.

68. See, for instance, Jonathan Last, "What Blogs Have Wrought," *WS*, September 27, 2004, 27–31.

69. Nicholas Lemann, "Fear and Favor," *New Yorker*, February 14/February 21, 2005 (double issue), 172.

70. As quoted in Robert Brent Toplin, *Radical Conservatism* (Lawrence: University Press of Kansas, 2006), 273.

Conclusion   When Extremism Becomes a Virtue

1. George H. Nash, *The Conservative Intellectual Movement in America* (1976; reprint, Wilmington, Del.: ISI, 2006), 556.

2. For a fine (albeit too long) treatment of the libertarian side of the conservative mind, see Brian Doherty, *Radicals for Capitalism* (New York: Public Affairs, 2007).

3. For an important disquisition on the rebel, see Albert Camus, *The Rebel* (New York: Vintage, 1956).

4. Alan Wolfe, "Why Conservatives Can't Govern," *Washington Monthly* (July/August 2006): 32–40.

5. See for example, David Gerlenter, "Bush's Greatness," *WS*, September 13, 2004, 21–23; Andrew Ferguson, "The Birthplace of Bush Paranoia," *WS*, October 25, 2004, 23–38.

6. See Stephen Macedo, *Liberal Virtues* (New York: Oxford University Press, 1990); William Galston, *Liberal Purposes* (Cambridge: Cambridge University Press, 1991); Stephen Holmes, *Passions and Constraints* (Chicago: University of Chicago Press, 1995); and, to a lesser extent, Richard Rorty, *Contingency, Irony, and Solidarity* (Cambridge: Cambridge University Press, 1989).

7. See Kevin Mattson, *When America Was Great: The Fighting Faith of Postwar Liberalism* (New York: Routledge, 2004).

Index

abortion, 94, 117, 123

absolutism. *See* extremism

academe, 37–38, 101, 136, 140; conservative criticism of, 60, 62, 64–65, 117–118; Horowitz's activism against, 5–6, 118–121. See also *God and Man at Yale* (Buckley); universities

Academic Bill of Rights (ABOR), 118–119, 120–121, 124, 130

academic freedom, 8, 34, 37, 67, 75, 103; Buckley and, 119, 130; neoconservatives and, 80–81; SAF and, 118, 120

activism. *See* Academic Bill of Rights (ABOR); protests

Adorno, Theodor, 108–109

Advertisements for Myself (Mailer), 88, 90

The Affluent Society (Galbraith), 81

African Americans, 89, 99. *See also* civil rights movement

Agnew, Spiro, 125–126

American Enterprise Institute, 19

American Mercury, 43

antiauthoritarianism, 135–136. *See also* rebellion; states' rights

anticommunism, 26, 38–39, 69, 78, 84. *See also* communism

anti-elitism, 99, 108–109. *See also* populism

anti-intellectualism, 1, 116, 131, 132, 135, 136; of conservative intellectuals, 35, 42–47, 119, 130, 148n57; of conservatives in 1960s and 1970s, 81, 87, 90–91, 103–104, 154n60; in 1950s culture, 46

Anton, Michael, 110–111

apocalyptic mindset, 22, 24, 70–71, 117, 129, 133; Cold War and, 26, 29, 130. *See also* war, mindset of

Armies of the Night (Mailer), 126

Army-McCarthy hearings (1954), 41

The Art of Political War: How Republicans Can Fight to Win (Horowitz), 100, 155–156n4

Atlas Shrugged (Rand), 31

baby boomers, 64

Backward and Upward (Brooks), 111

Barnes, Fred, 1–2, 110, 116, 136

Barton, Bruce, 35

Beat writers, 37, 57, 64, 87

Bell, Daniel, 22, 61, 81

Berman, Ronald, 63

Paglia, Camille, 99
Partisan Review, 90
Pells, Richard, 16
Penley, Constance, 109
Philadelphia Society, 73
Phillips, Kevin, 93–94, 96
pluralism, 135
Pocket Books, 127
Podhoretz, John, 108, 110
Podhoretz, Norman, 18, 62, 79, 94, 95–96, 115, 152–153n34; anti-intellectualism of, 104; Brooks compared, 111; "new sensibility" of, 86–92, 99, 136, 154n60
political power, 120–121
popular culture, 14, 108, 109–111, 129, 136
populism, 18, 35, 93, 96, 131, 135; anti-intellectualism and, 46–47; cultural studies and, 109–110; economic, 138; of Horowitz, 119; limitations of, 138–139; of *National Review,* 72; neoconservative criticism of, 95; Old Right and, 77; populist aggression and, 2–3; in the South, 51–52; *vs.* republicanism, 85–86. *See also* cultural populism
Port Huron Statement (SDS), 65, 66
postmodern conservatism, 18, 63, 96, 97–132, 134; academe and, 117–121; anti-intellectualism and, 103–104, 116, 119; Brooks and, 111–114; cultural fragmentation, 105–106, 107; endgame of, 129–132; Horowitz and, 97, 98, 100–101,

117, 118–121; P. Johnson and, 124–125; B. Kristol and, 108, 115–116; media and, 125–129; 1960s cultural radicalism and, 99–100, 102, 122, 130; popular culture and, 108, 109–111; science and, 121–125; "Second Thoughts" conference and, 97–99; "smashmouth" tendency of, 107, 136; "vaudeville" performance in, 9–10, 106
poststructuralism, 103
The Power Elite (Mills), 36
Powers, John, 5
professionalism, 140
A Program for Conservatives (Kirk), 46–47
Project for a New American Century, 115
protests: anti-draft activism, 77; anti-Vietnam War, 66, 78, 93; student, 72, 74, 75–76, 80–81, 118, 120; by YAF'ers, 67, 77
Public Interest, 79, 80, 84
public language, 139–140

racism, 53, 89
radicalism, 98, 119–120, 130; "new," 57, 60–61
radio talk shows, 106, 127, 128
Ramparts, 98
Rand, Ayn, 31, 45, 121, 134–135
Randolph, A. Philip, 52
Randolph of Roanoke (Kirk), 48
Ransom, John Crowe, 16
rationality, 139–140
Reagan, Ronald, 68, 92, 97
"Reagan Revolution," 99

About the Author

KEVIN MATTSON is Connor Study Professor of contemporary history at Ohio University. His work examines the intersection between politics and the world of ideas in numerous books, including, most recently, *Upton Sinclair and the Other American Century* (2006). He is also the author of *When America Was Great: The Fighting Faith of Postwar Liberalism*; *Engaging Youth: Combating the Apathy of Young Americans Toward Politics*; *Intellectuals in Action: The Origins of the New Left and Radical Liberalism*; and *Creating a Democratic Public: The Struggle for Urban Participatory Democracy during the Progressive Era*. He is the editor of *Liberalism for a New Century*; *Steal This University! The Rise of the Corporate University and the Academic Labor Movement*; and *Democracy's Moment*. His essays have appeared in the *New York Times Book Review*, the *Washington Post Book World*, the *Nation*, the *American Prospect*, *Common Review*, the *Baffler*, and *Chronicle Review*. He is presently an affiliated scholar at the Center for American Progress, active in the American Association of University Professors (AAUP), and on the editorial board of *Dissent* magazine.